Math Series

TRIGONOMETRY

by Stephen B. Jahnke

Book cover design by Kathy Kifer

Dedicated to Joy and my parents.

Special thanks to Kim Leeds, Harry Jahnke, Joy Leal, and Cecily Cleveland
for proofreading and suggestions.

Published by
Garlic Press
605 Powers St.
Eugene, OR 97402

ISBN 0-931993-45-8
Order Number GP-045

Printed in China
www.garlicpress.com

CONTENTS

Skills Review

In the next few pages we will review some math skills that will help later in this book. These skills, outlined below, can be easily learned even if you have never been introduced to them before.

Converting a Fraction into a Decimal

To convert a fraction into a decimal, divide the numerator by the denominator.

•Example 1:

Convert the following into decimals: (a.) $\frac{6}{5}$ (b.) $\frac{9.375}{12.5}$

Solution: (a.) $\frac{6}{5}$ = 6 ÷ 5 = 1.2   Using a calculator.

(b.) $\frac{9.375}{12.5}$ = 9.375 ÷ 12.5 = 0.75   Using a calculator.

Skills Review. Exercise 1. Convert the following into decimals.

1. $\frac{3}{4}$ 2. $\frac{5}{16}$ 3. $\frac{2.5}{4}$ 4. $\frac{6}{12.5}$ 5. $\frac{100.2}{4.36}$

Acute, Obtuse, and Right Angles

Angles which measure 90° are called **right angles**. Angles smaller than 90° are called **acute angles**. Angles larger than 90° are called **obtuse angles**.

Acute Angle   Right Angle   Obtuse Angle

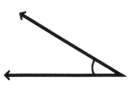  

Smaller than 90°   90° angle   Larger than 90°

Skills Review. Exercise 2. Identify each angle as acute, right, or obtuse.

1. 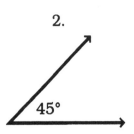 2. 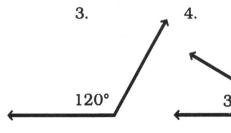 3. 4.

5. A 15° angle is an _____ angle.
6. A 90° angle is a _____ angle.

The Subtraction Principle

The Subtraction Principle states:

If   x + a = b
then   x = b - a

Example 2:

If x + 3 = 25, then what is x ?

Solution: x + 3 = 25
                  x = 25 - 3   Subtracting 3 from 25.
                  x = 22

The above answer, namely x = 22, is correct since 22 + 3 = 25.

Skills Review. Exercise 3. Solve by the Subtraction Principle.

1. x + 7 = 10   3. 9 = x + 4   5. B + 49 = 100
2. Y + 3 = 11   4. 22 = A + 11   6. 65 = 19 + B

2

Approximately Equal

The symbol ≈ means "approximately equal to" and is used to show that a number has been rounded.

Example 3

> Round 5.738 to two decimal points.
>
> Solution: 5.738 ≈ 5.74

Skills Review.   Exercise 4.

1. Round each to two decimal places.

   A. 0.237 ≈ _____   B. 15.314 ≈ _____   C. 180.016 ≈ _____

2. Round each to one decimal place.

   A. 4.18 ≈ _____   B. 79.62 ≈ _____   C. 8.591 ≈ _____

Square Roots

The following examples demonstrate how to calculate square roots.

Example 3:

> Calculate the following square roots.
>
> a. $\sqrt{9}$ Answer: $\sqrt{9}$ = 3, since 3 x 3 = 9.
>
> b. $\sqrt{64}$ Answer: $\sqrt{64}$ = 8, since 8 x 8 = 64.
>
> c. $\sqrt{7}$ Answer: $\sqrt{7}$ ≈ 2.65 by using the $\sqrt{}$ button
>   on your calculator and then rounding.

Skills Review. Exercise 5. Calculate the following square roots. Use a Calculator where necessary (and round to two decimal places).

A. $\sqrt{4}$ C. $\sqrt{100}$ E. $\sqrt{3}$ G. $\sqrt{11}$

B. $\sqrt{25}$ D. $\sqrt{1}$ F. $\sqrt{5}$ H. $\sqrt{81}$

The Square Root Principle

All the variables in this section represent positive numbers.

The **Square Root Principle** (for positive numbers) says:

$$
\begin{array}{l}
\text{If} \quad x^2 = p \\
\text{then} \quad x = \sqrt{p}
\end{array}
$$

Example 1 and 2 should clarify this process.

Example 1:

If $x^2 = 16$, then find x.

Solution: $x^2 = 16$
            $x = \sqrt{16}$ by the Square Root Principle.
            $x = 4$

The result of Example 1, namely x = 4, is correct because $(4)^2 = 16$.

Example 2:

If $x^2 = 10$, find x.

Solution: $x^2 = 10$
            $x = \sqrt{10}$ Square Root Principle.
            $x \approx 3.16$ Using a calculator and then rounding.

4

Skills Review. Exercise 6. solve each of the following by the Square Root Principle. Use a calculator when necessary.

1. $x^2 = 9$ 4. $x^2 = 7$ 7. $c^2 = 15$

2. $x^2 = 25$ 5. $c^2 = 4$ 8. $A^2 = 64$

3. $16 = x^2$ 6. $36 = c^2$ 9. $10 = B^2$

Facts About Triangles

Trigonometry is one of the most important topics in mathematics. Trigonometry is used in many fields including physics, engineering, architecture, surveying, aviation, navigation, and in the software of computer graphics programs.

Moreover, trigonometry has historical significance. In ancient Greece, astronomers used it in many calculations. From ancient Egypt to modern times, trigonometry has been used to partition land into properties. Also, until the use of satellites, the most accurate maps were constructed using trignometry.

The word *trigonometry* means triangle measurement. It is appropriate, therefore, that we should start with some facts about triangles.

Triangles

Every triangle contains three angles. The measurements of these angles always total 180°. (Refer to Figure A and B below.) Figure B contains a 90°angle, also called a **right angle**. Right angles are shown by drawing a square corner as in Figure B.

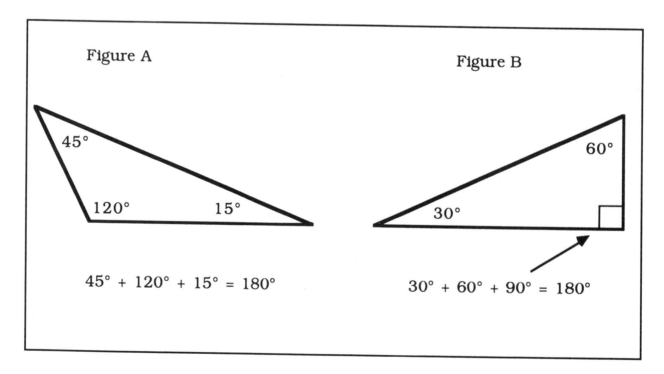

Figure A

45°

120°   15°

45° + 120° + 15° = 180°

Figure B

60°

30°

30° + 60° + 90° = 180°

If the measure of an angle is not known, then that angle is labeled by using a letter from the Greek alphabet. For example, in Figure C one of the angles is labeled by the Greek letter theta, θ. In Figure D, the angles are labeled as alpha, α; beta, β; and, gamma, γ.

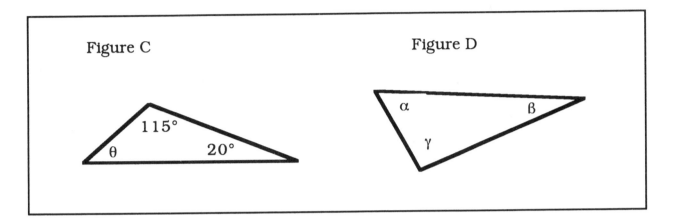

Example 1:

Determine the measurement of angle θ in Figure C.

Solution: The three angles must total 180°. The two known angles, 115° and 20°, already total 135°. Therefore, θ must be 45°, since 180° - 135° = 45°. (Check. 45° + 115° + 20° = 180°)

The **sides** of a triangle can be labeled by using letters from the English alphabet. (See Figure E) An **opposite side** is a side that is across from a particular angle. For instance, in Figure E, side A is opposite angle α.

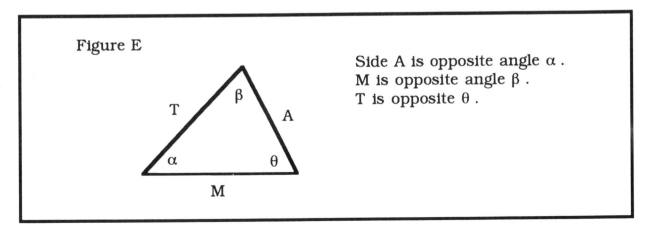

7

Example 2:

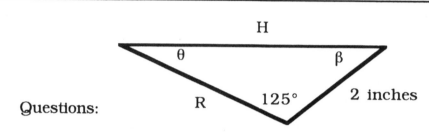

Questions:

a. Side H is opposite which angle?
b. What side is opposite angle θ?
c. R is the opposite side to which angle?

Answers:

a. H is opposite the 125° angle.
b. The side labeled "2 inches" is opposite θ .
c. β .

Triangles. Exercise 1.

1. The angles in a triangle must total_____°.

2. In each triangle below, find the measure of the unknown angle.

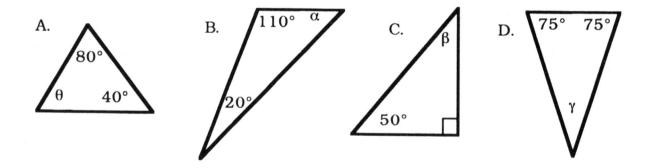

8

3. Use the two triangles below to answer these questions:

    A. Side A is opposite what angle?

    B. What side is opposite the 80° angle.

    C. The 3 cm side is opposite which angle?

    D. Y is opposite which angle?

    E. What side is opposite the right angle?

    F. X is the opposite side to which angle?

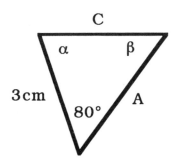 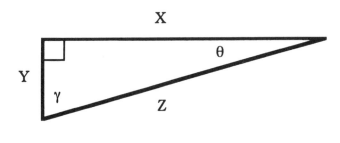

4. Fill in the blanks:

    A. Greek letters are used to label _____ .

    B. English letters are use to label _____ .

5. Fill in the blanks:

    A. 1 is opposite _____ .

    B. 2 is opposite _____ .

    C. $\sqrt{3}$ is opposite _____ .

    D. The measure of θ is _____ .

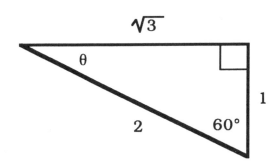

Right Triangles

A triangle is called a **right triangle** if it contains a 90° angle (a right angle).

For example:

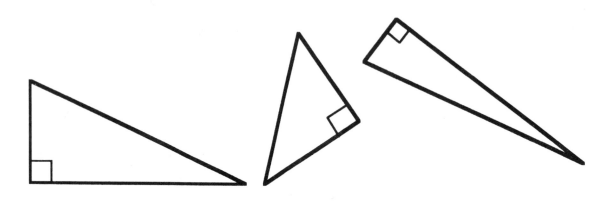

The side opposite the 90° angle is called the **hypotenuse**. The hypotenuse (hyp) is labeled in each triangle below.

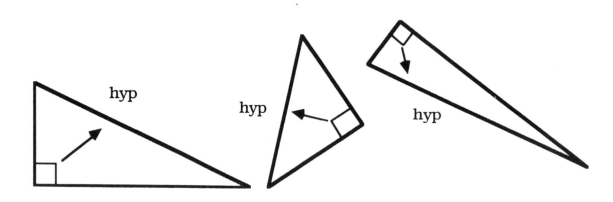

The remaining sides are called **legs**. The legs are labeled in each triangle.

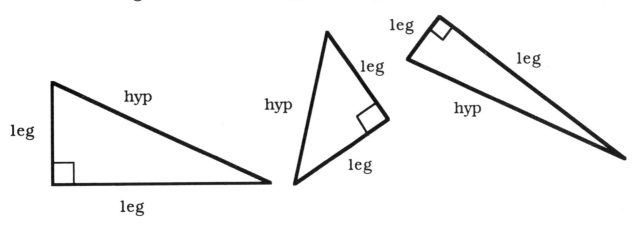

Right Triangles.   Exercise 2.

1. Which of the following are right triangles?

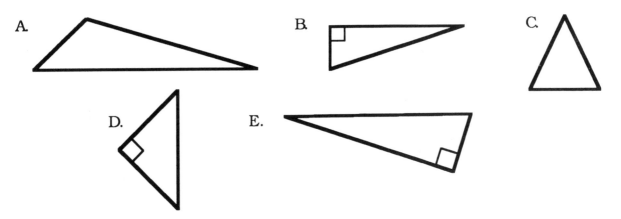

2. In each of the following, label each side appropriately as either a
   hypotenuse or a leg.

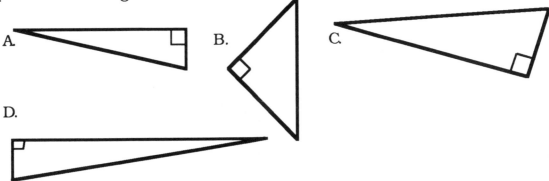

3. Given 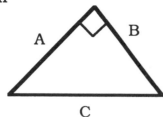 and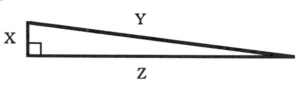

    A. Side A is called a _____ .

    B. Side B is called a _____ .

    C. Side C is called a _____ .

    D. Which of sides X, Y, or Z is the hypotenuse?

4. Given the triangle: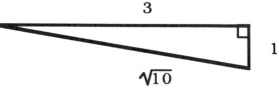

    A. The hypotenuse is _____ .

    B. The legs are _____ and _____ .

5. Fill in the blanks.

    A. The hypotenuse of any right triangle is the side _____ the 90° angle.

    B. The longest side of any right triangle is the _____ . (Hint: look back at the examples)

    C. Given the triangle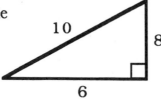

        (1.) The hypotenuse is _____ .

        (2.) The legs are _____ and _____ .

        (3.) The hypotenuse squared is _____ .

        (4.) The legs squared are _____ and _____ ,

        (5.) Add the answers in part (4.) together.

        (6.) Is the answer to part (5.) the same as the answer to part 3?

        The next section will show that this is no coincidence.

The Pythagorean Theorem

This section shows you how to find the length of the hypotenuse whenever the lengths of each leg are already known. To do this, however, we need to borrow a fact from geometry called the **Pythagorean Theorem**.

The Pythagorean Theorem

In any right triangle, if C is the length of the hypotenuse and if A and B are the length of the legs,

then $\mathbf{C^2 = A^2 + B^2}$.

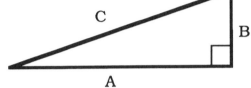

The formula in the above theorem, namely $C^2 = A^2 + B^2$, is used to calculate the length of the hypotenuse, C, whenever the lengths of the legs, A and B, are already known.

Example 1:

Use the formula, $C^2 = A^2 + B^2$, to calculate the length of the hypotenuse, C.

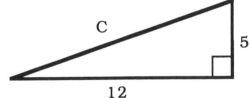

Answer: The legs are 12 and 5, so we can replace A and B with 12 and 5 (in any order) to get:

$$C^2 = A^2 + B^2$$
$$C^2 = 12^2 + 5^2$$

Now, square the 12 and 5. Then add the results together:

$$C^2 = 12^2 + 5^2$$
$$C^2 = 144 + 25$$
$$C^2 = 169$$

Finally, find C by taking the square root of 169:

$$C^2 = 169$$
$$C = \sqrt{169} \qquad \text{By the Square Root Principle (page 4).}$$
$$C = 13$$

In other words, if the legs are 12 and 5, then the hypotenuse must be 13.

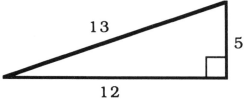

In the above example, we replaced A with 12 and B with 5. We could have gotten the same answer by instead replacing A with 5 and B with 12. The order of replacement makes no difference.

Example 2:

Calculate the length of the hypotenuse C.

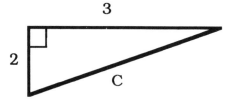

Answer: The legs are 2 and 3. Therefore,

$$C^2 = A^2 + B^2$$
$$C^2 = 2^2 + 3^2$$
$$C^2 = 4 + 9$$
$$C^2 = 13$$
$$C = \sqrt{13}$$

$C \approx 3.61$ because $\sqrt{13} \approx 3.61$ by using a calculator.

14

In other words, when the legs are 2 and 3, then the hypotenuse must be $\sqrt{13} \approx 3.61$. That is,

3   OR   3

2   $\sqrt{13}$ 2   3.61

Pythagorean Theorem.   Exercise 3.

1. For each of the following triangles, use the formula $C^2 = A^2 + B^2$ to find the hypotenuse as in Examples 1 and 2.

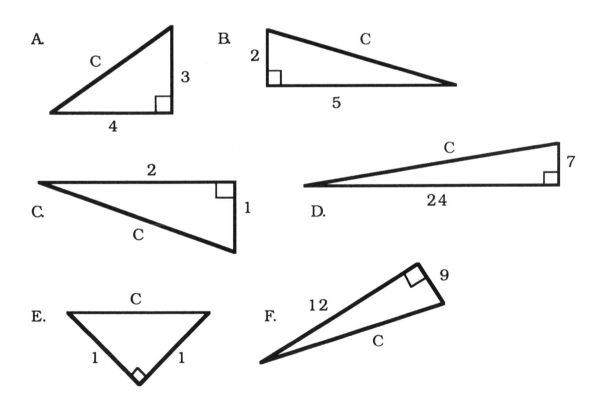

A.
C
3
4

B.
2
C
5

C.
2
C
1

D.
C
7
24

E.
C
1   1

F.
12
9
C

2. Do Example 1 again, but this time replace A with 5 and B with 12. Do you get the same answer as in Example 1?

Finding the Length of a Leg

In the previous section, we calculated the length of the hypotenuse using the formula, $C^2 = A^2 + B^2$, where C = hypotenuse and A and B represent the legs.

Interestingly, this same formula can be used to find the length of an unknown leg whenever the other leg and hypotenuse are known.

Example 1:

Use $C^2 = A^2 + B^2$ to find the length of leg B in this triangle.

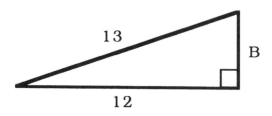

Answer: The hypotenuse is 13, so C = 13. The given leg is 12, so A = 12. Replacing C with 13 and A with 12, we get:

$$C^2 = A^2 + B^2$$
$$13^2 = 12^2 + B^2 \qquad \text{Since C = hyp = 13 and A = leg = 12.}$$
$$169 = 144 + B^2$$
$$169 - 144 = B^2 \qquad \text{The Subtraction Principle (page 2).}$$
$$25 = B^2$$
$$\sqrt{25} = B \qquad \text{The Square Root Principle (page 4).}$$
$$5 = B \quad \text{so } B = 5$$

Example 2:

Find the length of the unknown leg.

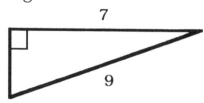

Answer: The hypotenuse is 9, so C = 9. Since the unknown leg is not labeled, we can label it ourselves with 'A' or 'B'. (It does not matter which letter we use.) Let's choose to label it as A.

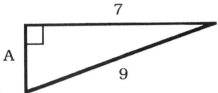

The given leg is 7, so B = 7. Then,

$$C^2 = A^2 + B^2$$
$$9^2 = A^2 + 7^2 \qquad \text{Since C = hyp = 9 and B = leg = 7.}$$
$$81 = A^2 + 49$$
$$81 - 49 = A^2 \qquad \text{By subtracting 49.}$$
$$32 = A^2$$
$$\sqrt{32} = A \quad \text{so} \quad A = \sqrt{32} \approx 5.66 \text{ by a calculator.}$$

Finding the Length of a Leg. Exercise 4.

1. Use $C^2 = A^2 + B^2$ to find the unknown leg in each triangle.

A.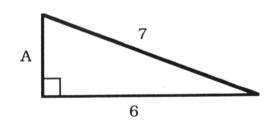

B.

C.

D.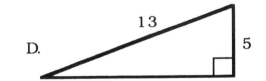

E.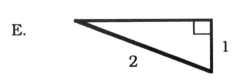

F.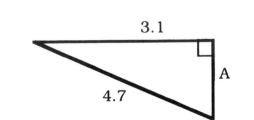

17

Pythagorean Formulas

You are already familiar with the formula $C^2 = A^2 + B^2$ where C = hypotenuse (Figure 1 below). This section shows how to write similar formulas when the sides of the triangle are labeled with letters other than A, B, and C (Figures 2 and 3 below).

Figure 1

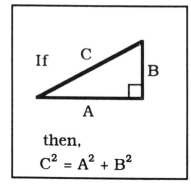

If

then,
$$C^2 = A^2 + B^2$$

Figure 2

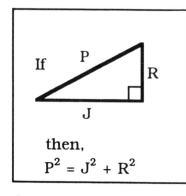

If

then,
$$P^2 = J^2 + R^2$$

Figure 3

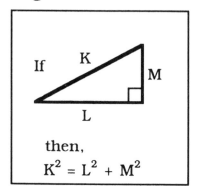

If

then,
$$K^2 = L^2 + M^2$$

Notice in each of Figures 1, 2, and 3 that the hypotenuse squared (that is, C^2, P^2, or K^2) is always by itself on one side of the equal sign and that the legs squared are always on the other side. In other words,

$$(hyp)^2 = (leg)^2 + (leg)^2$$

regardless of which letters are chosen to represent the sides.

Example 1

Write an appropriate formula for this triangle.

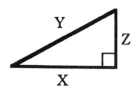

Answer: The hypotenuse is Y and the legs are X and Z.
Therefore, $Y^2 = X^2 + Z^2$.

Example 2

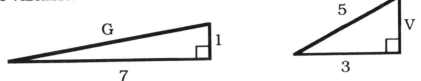

In each triangle, write an appropriate formula, then solve for the variable.

Answers. In the first triangle, the hypotenuse = G and the legs are 7 and 1. Hence:

$$G^2 = 7^2 + 1^2$$
$$G^2 = 49 + 1$$
$$G^2 = 50$$
$$G = \sqrt{50} \approx 7.1$$

In the second triangle, the hypotenuse = 5 and the legs are 3 and V. Hence:

$$5^2 = 3^2 + V^2$$
$$25 = 9 + V^2$$
$$25 - 9 = V^2$$
$$16 = V^2$$
$$\sqrt{16} = V \quad \text{so} \quad V = \sqrt{16} = 4$$

Pythagorean Formulas. Exercise 5.

1. Write an appropriate formula for each triangle.

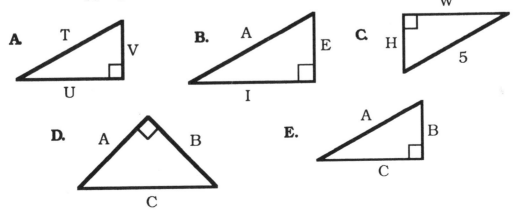

2. Write an appropriate formula, then solve for the variable.

A.
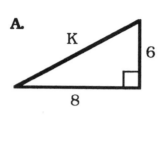

B.
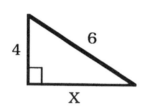

C.
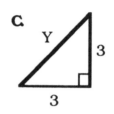

D.
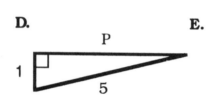

E.
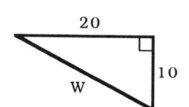

F.

20

Applications

The previous sections discussed methods for finding the unknown hypotenuse or leg of right triangles. Here, we offer interesting situations that use these procedures.

Example 1:

Kate is designing a tent for a company that makes camping equipment. She wants the tent to be 4 feet tall. She also wants the tent to have 3 feet between its entrance zipper and the ground peg.

What length, C, of fabric must the company use to reach from the top of the tent to the ground peg?

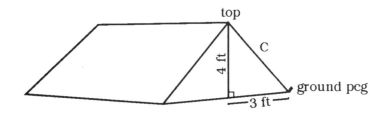

Answer: In the above picture, we notice a right triangle with hypotenuse C and legs 3 feet and 4 feet.

Hence:

$$C^2 = 3^2 + 4^2$$
$$C^2 = 9 + 16$$
$$C^2 = 25$$
$$C = \sqrt{25}$$
$$C = 5$$

The company must use 5 feet of fabric to reach from the top of the tent to the ground peg.

The next Example is solved by finding the unknown leg of the right triangle.

Example 2:

Jerry is a surveyor for a map making company. As a part of his job, he needs to determine the length of a swamp (see picture). The swamp is too marshy to measure its length directly. Fortunately, he already knows that one end of the swamp is 7 miles from a nearby town. The other end of the swamp is 3 miles from the town and this distance makes a right triangle with the swamp. How long is the swamp?

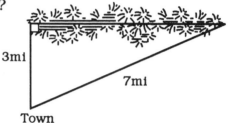

3mi

7mi

Town

Answer: The hypotenuse of this right triangle is 7 miles. One leg is 3 miles. The other leg is the length of the swamp, which we can call x .

Hence:
$$7^2 = 3^2 + x^2$$
$$49 = 9 + x^2$$
$$49 - 9 = x^2$$
$$40 = x^2$$
$$\sqrt{40} = x \qquad\qquad \text{so} \quad x = \sqrt{40} \approx 6.32$$

The swamp is 6.32 miles long.

Applications. Exercise 6. Use the methods of finding the unknown hypotenuse or leg to solve these problems.

1. Mollie is designing an A-frame house that is 12 yards tall
   (see Figure A on next page). The distance from the door
   to a corner is 5 yards. Find the length of the roof marked C.

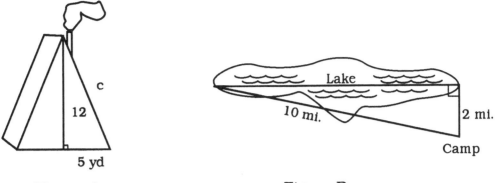

c

12

5 yd

Figure A

Lake

10 mi.

2 mi.

Camp

Figure B

2. A surveyor wishes to know the length of a lake. She knows the distance from her camp to each side of the lake (Figure B). The distance from her camp to the near side of the lake makes a right angle with the lake's length. How long is the lake?

3. Derick wants to make a wheel chair ramp from his driveway to the top of his front porch. His porch is 1 foot high. The distance from his porch to his driveway is 16 feet (Figure C). How long will the incline be?

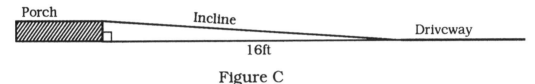

Porch

Incline

Driveway

16ft

Figure C

4. It takes Sue 10 minutes to walk to the store from her house if she cuts through the field (see Figure D). On rainy days she uses the sidewalk. It takes her 5 minutes to walk from her house to the corner. How long does it take Sue to walk from the corner to the store?

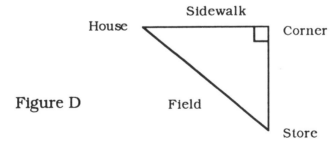

Sidewalk

House

Corner

Figure D

Field

Store

5. You are installing cable television to people's homes. On your last stop of the day, you notice that you have only 40 feet of cable left. The nearest telephone pole is 25 ft from the house and the pole is 30 feet high (See Figure E). Do you have enough cable?

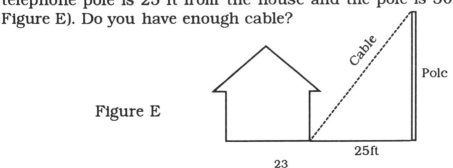

Cable

Pole

Figure E

25ft

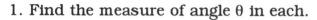

1. Find the measure of angle θ in each.

A.
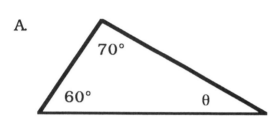
70°
60°
θ

B.
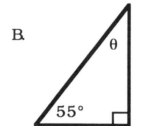
θ
55°

2. Use the triangle below to answer the following:

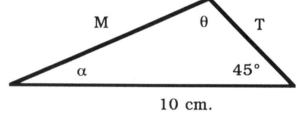

    A. Side T is opposite which angle?

    B. θ is opposite which side?

    C. Side M is opposite which angle?

M   θ   T

α   45°

10 cm.

3. Which of the two triangles in Problem 1 is a right triangle?

4. In the following triangle:

    A. The hypotenuse is labeled as _____.

    B. The legs are _____ and ____.

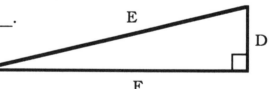

E

D

F

5. In each of the following, use the formula $C^2 = A^2 + B^2$ to find the unknown side.

A.
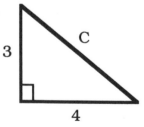
3
C
4

B.
2
7

C.
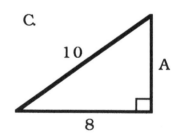
10
A
8

D.
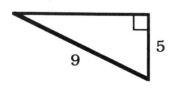
9
5

E.
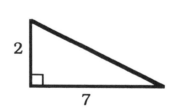
12
5
X

F.
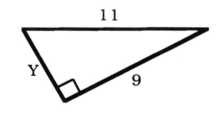
11
Y
9

24

6. Write an appropriate formula for this triangle.

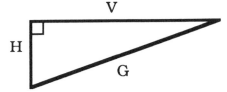

7. A 15 foot ladder is leaning against the side of a house. The bottom of the ladder is 2 feet from the base of the house. How high will the ladder reach on the house?

Trigonometric Ratios

This chapter discusses the sine, the cosine, and the tangent. Before explaining these terms, we wish to remind you of what the word **ratio** means.

Ratios

Finding the **ratio** of two numbers means to make a fraction by placing the first number in the numerator and the second number in the denominator.

Example 1:

A. Find the ratio of 5 to 8.	Answer $\frac{5}{8}$
B. Find the ratio of 6 to 12.	Answer $\frac{6}{12} = \frac{1}{2}$
C. Find the ratio of 12 to 6.	Answer $\frac{12}{6} = 2$
D. Find the ratio of x to y.	Answer $\frac{x}{y}$

Example B and C above emphasize that the order of the numbers is important.

Example 2

In a group of 30 men and 40 women, find:
A. The ratio of men to women.
B. The ratio of women to total.

Answers: A. $\frac{\text{men}}{\text{women}} = \frac{30}{40} = \frac{3}{4}$ B. $\frac{\text{women}}{\text{total}} = \frac{40}{70} = \frac{4}{7}$

Ratios. Exercise 1.

1. The ratio of 4 to 9 is _____.
2. The ratio of P to T is _____.
3. A rectangle has a length of 8 and a width of 2 find:
   A. The ratio of length to width;
   B. The ratio of width to length;
   C. The ratio of length to perimeter.

Opposite and Adjacent Sides

This section will help you understand the sine ratio, the cosine ratio, and the tangent ratio introduced in the next section.

Remember from the previous chapter that one angle in a right triangle is always 90°. The two remaining angles are called acute angles. If we pick one of these acute angles (at random) and label it with a Greek letter, say θ, then we will be able to distinguish one leg from the other leg.

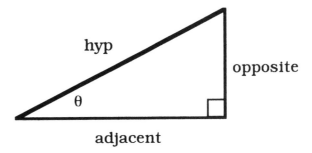

The leg that is nearest θ is called the **adjacent** leg or simply the adjacent side. The leg that is opposite θ is called the **opposite** leg or opposite side. θ is called the **reference angle**.

Example 1:

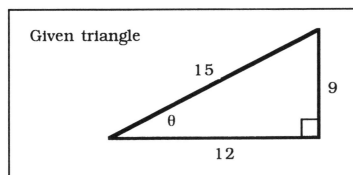

Given triangle

Questions:
1. What is the hypotenuse?
2. What is the opposite side to θ ?
3. What is the adjacent side to θ ?

Answers: 1. hyp = 15   2. opp = 9   3. adj = 12

Note: Only legs may be designated as adjacent to a given angle. Although the hypotenuse may occupy one of two adjacent positions, it is never called the adjacent side. It remains simply the hypotenuse.

The next example uses the same triangle as Example 1; however, this time the other acute angle is labeled as θ. We do this to emphasize the fact that either angle can be used as the reference angle in distinguishing one leg from the other.

Example 2:

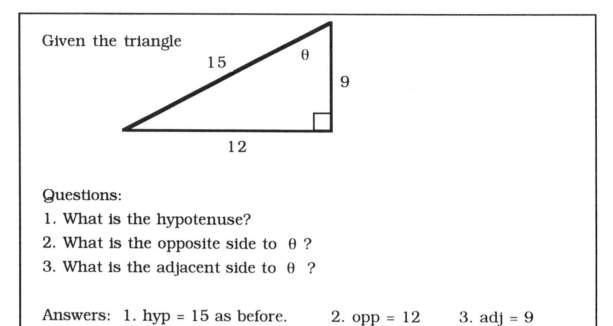

Given the triangle

15   θ

9

12

Questions:
1. What is the hypotenuse?
2. What is the opposite side to θ ?
3. What is the adjacent side to θ ?

Answers: 1. hyp = 15 as before.   2. opp = 12   3. adj = 9

The above two examples show thatference angle causes the opposite and adjacent legs to switch roles, where as the hypotenuse remains unchanged. The next example also demonstrates these facts.

Example 3:

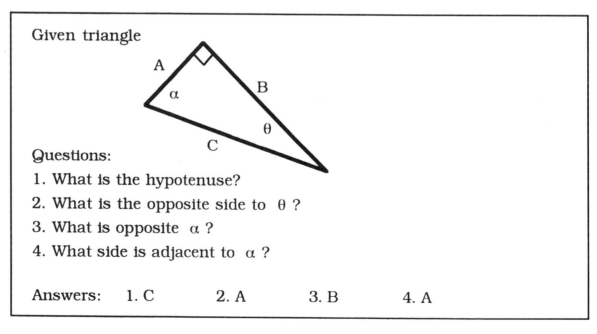

Given triangle

A

B

α

θ

C

Questions:
1. What is the hypotenuse?
2. What is the opposite side to θ ?
3. What is opposite α ?
4. What side is adjacent to α ?

Answers: 1. C   2. A   3. B   4. A

Opposite and Adjacent Sides. Exercise 2.

1. In each triangle below identify the legs opposite and adjacent to θ. Also identify the hypotenuse.

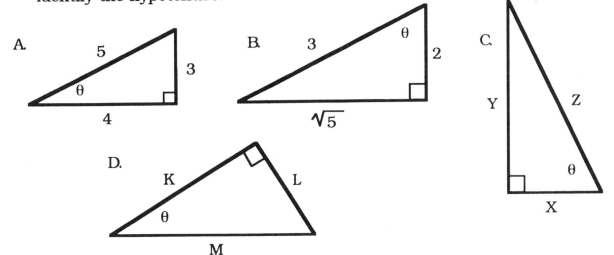

2. Given this triangle

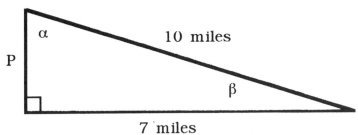

   Fill in the blanks.

   A. The hypotenuse is_____.
   B. The side adjacent to α   is _____.
   C. The side adjacent to β   is _____.
   D. P is _____ to angle α and _____ to angle β .
   E. What is the length of side P ?

The Sine, the Cosine, and the Tangent

In this section we will explain the meaning of three so-called trigonometric ratios: namely the sine, the cosine, and the tangent.

The Sine

The phrase *sine of angle* θ is abbreviated as $\sin \theta$ and means the ratio of the opposite side (opp) to the hypotenuse (hyp). In other words:

$$\sin \theta = \frac{\text{opp}}{\text{hyp}}$$

Example 1:

Find the sine of θ in this triangle

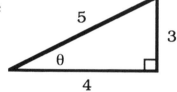

Answer: The hypotenuse is 5 and the opposite side is 3. Hence,

$$\sin \theta = \frac{\text{opp}}{\text{hyp}} = \frac{3}{5}$$

The Cosine

The phrase *cosine of angle* θ is abbreviated as $\cos \theta$ and means the ratio of the adjacent side (adj) to the hypotenuse (hyp). In other words:

$$\cos \theta = \frac{\text{adj}}{\text{hyp}}$$

Example 2:

Find the cosine of θ in this triangle

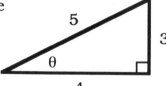

Answer: adj = 4 and hyp = 5. Hence,

$$\cos \theta = \frac{\text{adj}}{\text{hyp}} = \frac{4}{5}$$

The Tangent

The phrase *tangent of angle* θ is abbreviated as tan θ and means the ratio of the opposite side to the adjacent side. In other words:

$$\tan \theta = \frac{\text{opp}}{\text{adj}}$$

Example 3:

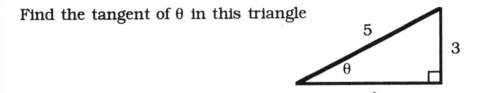

Find the tangent of θ in this triangle

Answer: opp = 3 and adj = 4. Hence,

$$\tan \theta = \frac{\text{opp}}{\text{adj}} = \frac{3}{4}$$

Notice that the same triangle was used in each of the above examples. Let's look at another example.

Example 4:

Given this triangle, find sin θ , cos θ , tan θ .

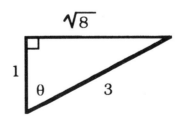

Answer: hyp = 3, opp = $\sqrt{8}$, and adj = 1.

Therefore, $\sin \theta = \dfrac{\text{opp}}{\text{hyp}} = \dfrac{\sqrt{8}}{3}$, $\cos \theta = \dfrac{\text{adj}}{\text{hyp}} = \dfrac{1}{3}$

and $\tan \theta = \dfrac{\text{opp}}{\text{adj}} = \dfrac{\sqrt{8}}{1} = \sqrt{8}$

The next example explains how to find the sine, cosine, and tangent when one side is not known. Also, it shows that other Greek letters besides θ can be used.

Example 5:

Given this triangle, find sin α , cos α , tan α .

3

α

2

Solution: Begin by using the Pythagorean Theorem to find the unknown side.

$$C^2 = A^2 + B^2$$
$$3^2 = 2^2 + B^2 \qquad \text{Since hyp = 3 and leg = 2.}$$
$$9 = 4 + B^2$$
$$9 - 4 = B^2$$
$$5 = B^2$$
$$\sqrt{5} = B \qquad \text{or}$$

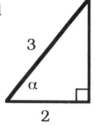

3

$\sqrt{5}$

α

2

Now, hyp = 3, opp = $\sqrt{5}$, and adj = 2. Hence,

$$\sin \alpha = \frac{\sqrt{5}}{3} \qquad\qquad \cos \alpha = \frac{2}{3} \qquad\qquad \tan \alpha = \frac{\sqrt{5}}{2}$$

It is a common practice to write the answers in <u>decimal form</u>. For instance, in the above example sin α was found to be $\frac{\sqrt{5}}{2}$ However, $\sqrt{5} \approx 2.236$ by using a calculator. Therefore,

$$\sin \alpha = \frac{\sqrt{5}}{2} \approx \frac{2.236}{3} \approx 0.745$$

In the previous examples we have calculated the sine, cosine, and tangent for angles labeled with Greek letters (like θ, or α). The next example shows this process applied to an angle measurement that is already known.

Example 6:

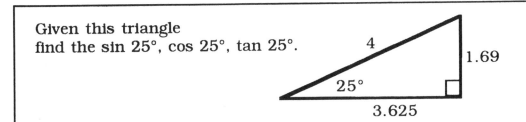

Given this triangle find the sin 25°, cos 25°, tan 25°.

4

1.69

25°

3.625

Answer: hyp = 4, opp = 1.69, adj = 3.62.

Hence: $\sin 25° = \frac{1.69}{4} \approx 0.422$, $\cos 25° = \frac{3.625}{4} \approx 0.906$,

and $\tan 25° = \frac{1.69}{3.625} \approx 0.466$.

Sine, Cosine, and Tangent. Exercise 3.

1. In each triangle below, find the sin θ, cos θ, and tan θ (as in Examples 1 through 4 above). **Leave the answers as fractions.**

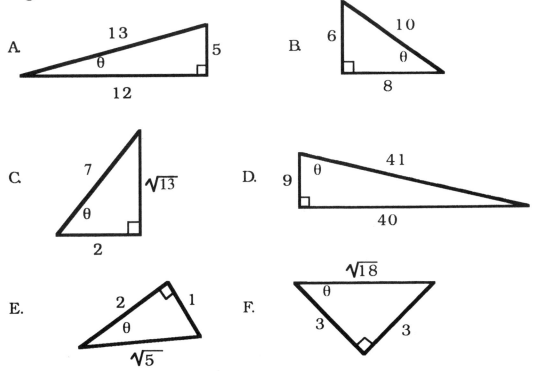

A. 13   5   θ   12

B. 6   10   θ   8

C. 7 $\sqrt{13}$ θ   2

D. 9   41   θ   40

E. 2   1   θ $\sqrt{5}$

F. $\sqrt{18}$ θ   3   3

2. In each of the following, find sin α , cos α , and tan α using the method in Example 5.

A.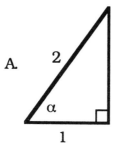

B.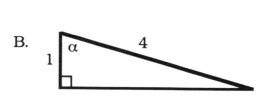

C.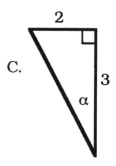

3. Convert the answers in Problem 2A above into decimal form.

4. Given this triangle, calculate each of the following (Hint: see Example 6).

A. sin 50°

B. cos 50°

C. tan 50°

D. sin β

E. cos β

F. The measure of angle β.

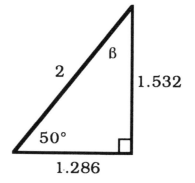

5. The sine, cosine, and tangent are called _____.

Three Facts

The last section explained the meaning of the three trigonometric ratios: sine, cosine, and tangent. This section demonstrates some important facts about these ratios.

Fact 1: The sine of any particular angle is always the same, regardless of the size of the triangle.

The next example clarifies Fact 1 by calculating sin 30° using three triangles.

Example 1:

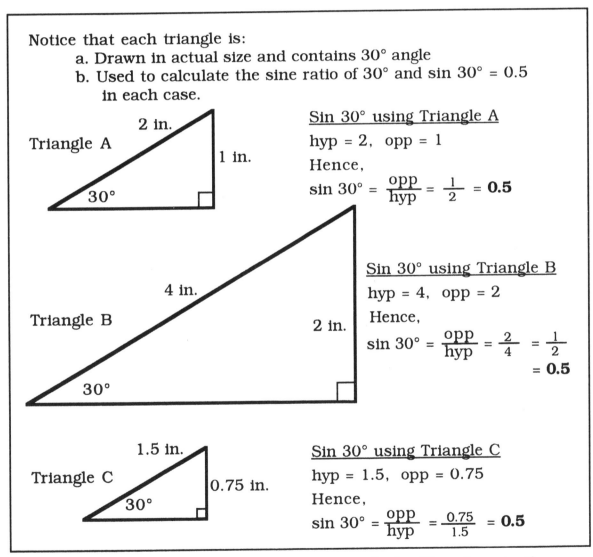

Notice that each triangle is:
    a. Drawn in actual size and contains 30° angle
    b. Used to calculate the sine ratio of 30° and sin 30° = 0.5
       in each case.

Triangle A — 2 in., 1 in., 30°

Sin 30° using Triangle A

hyp = 2, opp = 1

Hence,

$$\sin 30° = \frac{\text{opp}}{\text{hyp}} = \frac{1}{2} = \mathbf{0.5}$$

Triangle B — 4 in., 2 in., 30°

Sin 30° using Triangle B

hyp = 4, opp = 2

Hence,

$$\sin 30° = \frac{\text{opp}}{\text{hyp}} = \frac{2}{4} = \frac{1}{2} = \mathbf{0.5}$$

Triangle C — 1.5 in., 0.75 in., 30°

Sin 30° using Triangle C

hyp = 1.5, opp = 0.75

Hence,

$$\sin 30° = \frac{\text{opp}}{\text{hyp}} = \frac{0.75}{1.5} = \mathbf{0.5}$$

The sides in triangle B are double those in traingle A. Therefore, in the calculation of the sine ratios, **both** the numerator and denominator using B are double those using A. This causes the overall sine ratios to be identical (Since doubling **both** the top and bottom of a fraction does not affect its overall value).

The following example , like the last example, is meant to demonstrate that the sine of any particular angle is not affected by the size of the triangle.

Example 2:

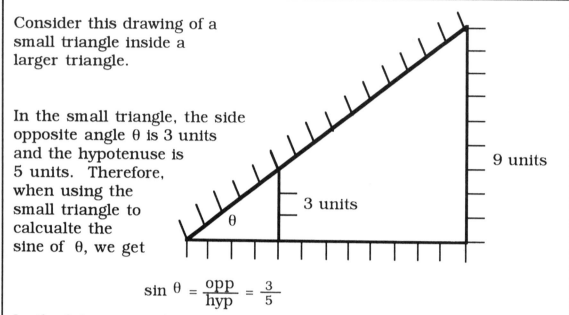

Consider this drawing of a small triangle inside a larger triangle.

In the small triangle, the side opposite angle θ is 3 units and the hypotenuse is 5 units. Therefore, when using the small triangle to calcualte the sine of θ, we get

9 units

3 units

θ

$$\sin \theta = \frac{opp}{hyp} = \frac{3}{5}$$

In the larger triangle, the side opposite angle θ is 9 units and the hypotenuse is 15 units. Therefore, when using the large triangle to calculate the sine of θ, we get

$$\sin \theta = \frac{opp}{hyp} = \frac{9}{15} = \frac{3}{5}$$

Hence the calculation of sin θ results in the same number, namely $\frac{3}{5}$, no matter which triangle is used.

Examples of the following two facts will be presented in Exercise 4 (see problems 1 and 2).

Fact 2: The cosine of any particular angle is always the same, regardless of the size of the triangle.

Fact 3: The tangent of any particular angle is always the same, regardless of the size of the triangle.

Three Facts. Exercise 4.

1. Answer these questions by referring back to the figure and angle θ of Example 2.

    A. Use the small triangle to calculate $\cos \theta = \dfrac{\text{adj}}{\text{hyp}}$.

    B. Use the larger triangle to calculate $\cos \theta$.

    C. What fact do Parts A and B demonstrate?

2. Refer to the triangles and angle θ of Example 2.

    A. Find tan θ using the small triangle.

    B. Find tan θ using the larger triangle.

    C. What fact do Parts A and B demonstate?

3. Consider the following figure of a smaller triangle inside a larger triangle.

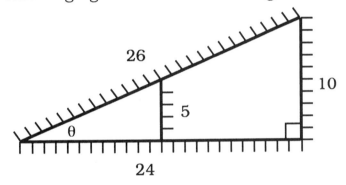

    A. Use the smaller triangle to find sin θ .

    B. Use the larger triangle to find sin θ .

    C. Use the smaller triangle to find cos θ .

    D. Use the larger triangle to find cos θ .

    E. Find tan θ of both triangles.

    F. What facts do Parts A through E demonstrate?

4. Find tan 45° using each actual size figure below.

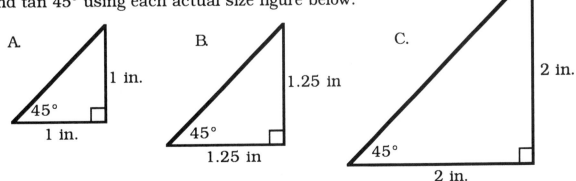

D. What fact does Part A, B, and C demonstrate?

5. This triangle contains a 30 ° angle.

hyp

opp

30°

   A. Use a ruler to measure the hypotenuse and opposite side to the nearest quarter inch.

   B. Write the measurements of Part A as decimals.
      (Hint: $\frac{1}{4}$ inch = 0.25 inch)

   C. Use the decimals in Part B to calculate sin 30°. Does your result agree with Example 1?

6. Use the Pythagorean Theorem (That is $C^2 = A^2 + B^2$, where C = hypotenuse) to find the hypotenuse of each triangle in Problem 4.

   A. Write each hypotenuse as a decimal. Round to three places.

   B. For each triangle calculate cos 45°. Round to three places.

   C. What fact is demonstrated in Parts A and C?

Tables

In the previous section you learned that trigonometric ratios do not depend on the size of the triangle. For instance, we observed that sin 30° always equals 0.5 regardless of the triangle size. Furthermore, Exercises 4 and 6 demonstrated that tan 45° = 1 and cos 45° ≈ 0.707.

Mathematicians have compiled hundreds of these kinds of observations in long tables called trigonometric tables. Shown below is a short trigonometric table. Here we have included a few of the more commonly occuring angles. Notice that the previously mentioned observations, namely sin 30° = 0.5 and tan 45° = 1 are included within this table.
(See Example 1 below.)

TRIGONOMETRIC TABLE

angle θ	sin θ	cos θ	tan θ
10°	0.174	0.985	0.176
15°	0.259	0.966	0.268
20°	0.342	0.940	0.364
30°	**0.5**	0.866	0.577
40°	0.643	0.766	0.839
45°	0.707	0.707	**1**
50°	0.766	0.643	1.192
60°	0.866	0.5	1.732
70°	0.940	0.342	2.747
75°	0.966	0.259	3.732
80°	0.985	0.174	5.671

The entries in this table have been rounded to three decimal places. The following example explains how to use the table.

Example 1:

Use the table to find:
     A. sin 30°   B. tan 45°   C. cos 75°

Answers: A. sin 30° = 0.5, since the *0.5* entry is in the same row as 30° and under the sin θ column.

B. tan 45° = 1, since the *1* entry is in the same row as 45° and under the tan θ column.

C. Similarly cos 75° = 0.259.

The table can also be used to find particular angles when their sines, cosines, or tangents are known.

Example 2:

A. If tan θ = 1.732, then find θ .
B. If sin θ = 0.707, then find θ.

Answers: A. 1.732 is the eighth entry under tan θ column. Start at this location and move across the table to the left to see that the corresponding angle is 60°.

B. Similarly, if sin = 0.707, then θ = 45°.

Tables. Exercise 5.

1. Refer to the table (page 39) to find each.

A. sin 10°	E. cos 75°	I. cos 60°
B. tan 10°	F. sin 75°	J. sin 30°
C. cos 45°	G. cos 15°	K. cos 30°
D. tan 80°	H. tan 50°	L. tan 75°

2. Answer the following using the table as in Example 2.

A. If sin θ= 0.259, then find θ.	E. If tan θ= 5.671, then find θ.
B. If cos θ= 0.866, then find θ.	F. If cos θ= 0.940, then find θ.
C. If tan θ= 1, then find θ.	G. If sin θ= 0.940, then find θ.
D. If sin θ= 0.707, then find θ.	H. If sin θ= 0.342, then find θ.

3. Compare the entries in the sin θ column to those in the cos θ column. What overall pattern can you see? Hint: See answers.

Calculators (optional)

This section is not necessary for understanding the rest of the book.

Here we merely point out that calculators having buttons marked *sin* , *cos* , and *tan* can be used in place of tables.

If you have such a calculator and you wish to use it instead of the tables provided in this book, then you must make sure the calculator is in *degree mode* . Different models of calculators work in different ways, so you will need to consult your manual to find out how to put your calculator into the degree mode.

Assuming your calculator is in degree mode, Example 1 explains how to find the sine of a specific angle.

Example 1:

> Find sin 15°.
>
> Solution: On some calculators you would enter 15 first, then press the *sin* button. On other calculators you will press *sin* first, then enter 15 and the equal sign button. Experiment with your calculator. You should get sin 15° = 0.258819 (Notice in our table on page 39, we have rounded this to sin 15° ≈ 0.259.).

The cosine and tangent buttons work in a similar way. For instance , cos 37° = 0.7986355.

Example 2 (on the next page) shows how to find the angle itself, when the sine of the angle is already known.

Example 2:

Given that sin θ= 0.839, find θ.

Solution: Many (but not all) calculators work as follows. Consult your manual if this process doesn't work.

Enter 0.839. Press a button that is labeled either *2ndF* or *Inv* , then press *sin* . You should get θ = 57.034672° or θ ≈ 57° rounded to the nearest degree.

The cosine and tangent buttons work in a similar way. For instance, if cos θ= 0.656, then θ ≈ 49°.

Calculators. Exercise 6.

1. Use a calculator as in Example 1. Round to three decimals.

      A. sin 45°   C. cos 3°   E. tan 12.5°

      B. tan 50°   D. sin 1°   F. cos 89.9°

2. Answer the following as in Example 2. Round to three decimals.

      A. If sin θ= 0.966, find θ.

      B. If cos θ = 0.1045, find θ.

      C. If tan θ = 114, find θ.

Review

1. In each triangle below, identify the legs opposite and adjacent to θ. Also identify the hypotenuse.

A.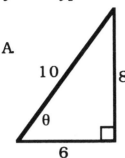

B.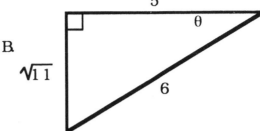

2. A. In the triangle of 1A, find sin θ, cos θ, and tan θ.
   B. In the triangle of 1B, find sin θ, cos θ, and tan θ.

3. Given this triangle, find:
   A. sin β
   B. cos β
   C. tan β
   D. sin α

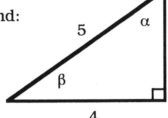

4. Given this triangle, calculate sin 30°.

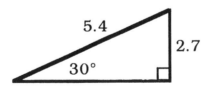

5. Fill in the blanks.
   A. The sine of any particular angle is always the same regardless of the _____ of the triangle.
   B. The tangent of a specific angle does not depend on the size of the _____.

6. Use the table or calculator to find the following.

   A. sin 10°   C. tan 45°   E. cos 45°
   B. cos 80°   D. sin 45°   F. tan 70°

43

7. Use the table (or calculator).

      A. If $\sin \theta = 0.985$, then find θ.

      B. If $\cos \beta = 0.707$, then find β.

      C. If $\tan \alpha = 0.364$, then find α.

8. Consider this figure of a small triangle inside of a larger triangle.

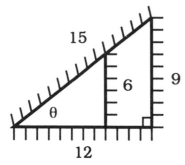

      A. Use the smaller triangle to find $\sin \theta$.

      B. Use the larger triangle to find $\sin \theta$.

      C. Find $\cos \theta$ using both triangles.

      D. Find $\tan \theta$ using both triangles.

9. In this triangle, find:

      A. $\sin \theta$

      B. $\cos \beta$

      C. $\sin \beta$

      D. $\cos \theta$

      E. $\tan \theta$

      F. $\tan \beta$

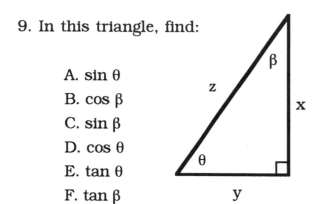

The goal of this chapter is to teach you to use the sine, cosine, and tangent to solve real-world problems. Before explaining this process, however, we need to remind you of a technique from arithmetic: *cross multiplying and dividing.*

Cross Multiply and Divide

When two fractions equal each other, any unknown numerator or denominator can be found. The following example demonstrates this process.

Example 1:

Find x when $\frac{x}{3} = \frac{2.1}{4}$

Process:

Step 1. Cross multiply (3)(2.1) as shown below.

$$\frac{x}{3} \diagup \frac{2.1}{4} \qquad (3)(2.1) = 6.3$$

Step 2. Divide the result of Step 1, namely 6.3, by the number which has not yet been used, namely 4, to get:

$$6.3 \div 4 = 1.575$$

Therefore x = 1.575.

In other words, if $\frac{x}{3} = \frac{2.1}{4}$, then x = (3)(2.1) ÷ 4 = 1.575

The next example shows what to do when one side of the equal sign is not in fraction form.

Example 2:

Find x when $\frac{9}{x} = 0.866$.

Process:

Step 1. 0.866 is the same as $\frac{0.866}{1}$. So, in the equation above place a 1 under the 0.866 to get:

$$\frac{9}{x} = \frac{0.866}{1}$$

Next, cross multiply and divide to get: $\frac{9}{x} = \frac{0.866}{1}$

$$x = (9 \times 1) \div 0.866$$
$$x = 9 \div 0.866$$
$$x \approx 10.39$$

Cross Multiply and Divide. Exercise 1.

1. Cross multiply and divide in each of the following.

A. $\frac{6}{8} = \frac{x}{4}$

B. $\frac{y}{2} = \frac{4.2}{3}$

C. $\frac{x}{12} = \frac{1}{3}$

D. $\frac{2.5}{1} = \frac{5}{c}$

E. $10 = \frac{2}{x}$

Hint: Rewrite 10 as $\frac{10}{1}$

F. $0.5 = \frac{x}{7}$

G. $0.707 = \frac{4}{P}$

H. $\frac{1}{y} = 0.364$

I. $\frac{x}{25} = 1$

Hint: Rewrite 1 as $\frac{1}{1}$

46

Finding an Unknown Side

Whenever one angle and one side of a right triangle are already known, the remaining sides can be found using the ratios: $\sin \theta = \dfrac{opp}{hyp}$, $\cos \theta = \dfrac{adj}{hyp}$, or $\tan \theta = \dfrac{opp}{adj}$.

Example 1:

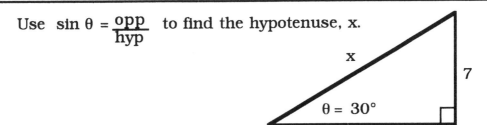

Use $\sin \theta = \dfrac{opp}{hyp}$ to find the hypotenuse, x.

Solution: $\theta = 30°$, opp = 7, and hyp = x.

Therefore, in $\sin \theta = \dfrac{opp}{hyp}$ replace θ with 30°, opp with 7, and hyp with x, to get:

$\sin \theta = \dfrac{opp}{hyp}$

$\sin 30° = \dfrac{7}{x}$ Since $\theta = 30°$, opp = 7, hyp = x.

$0.5 = \dfrac{7}{x}$ Since sin 30° = 0.5 from Trigonometric Table or by using a calcualtor.

$\dfrac{0.5}{1} = \dfrac{7}{x}$ Since $0.5 = \dfrac{0.5}{1}$

$x = 14$ By cross multiplying and dividing as in the previous section. That is (7 x 1) ÷ 0.5 = 14.

In other words, the hypotenuse = 14.

The above example used the sine ratio. The next example uses the cosine.

Example 2:

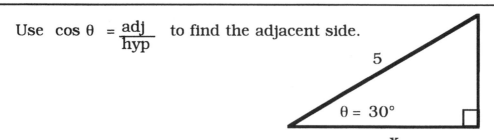

Use $\cos \theta = \dfrac{adj}{hyp}$ to find the adjacent side.

Answer: $\theta = 30°$, adj = x, and hyp = 5.   Therefore:

$$\cos \theta = \frac{adj}{hyp}$$

$$\cos 30° = \frac{x}{5}$$ Since $\theta = 30°$, adj = x, hyp = 5.

$$0.866 \overset{=}{} \frac{x}{5}$$ Since cos 30° = 0.866 from the table or by calcualtor.

$$\frac{0.866}{1} = \frac{x}{5}$$

$$x = (0.866)(5) \div 1$$ Cross multiply and Divide.

$$x = 4.33$$

The next example makes use of the tangent.

Example 3:

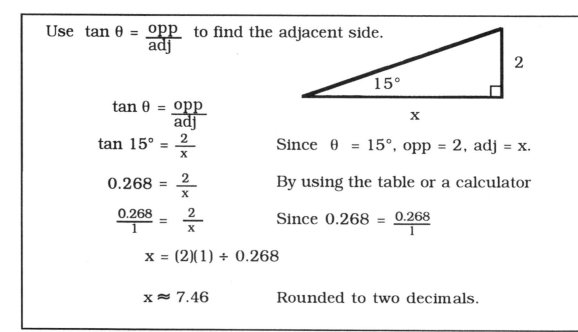

Use $\tan \theta = \dfrac{opp}{adj}$ to find the adjacent side.

$$\tan \theta = \frac{opp}{adj}$$

$$\tan 15° = \frac{2}{x}$$ Since $\theta = 15°$, opp = 2, adj = x.

$$0.268 = \frac{2}{x}$$ By using the table or a calculator

$$\frac{0.268}{1} = \frac{2}{x}$$ Since $0.268 = \frac{0.268}{1}$

$$x = (2)(1) \div 0.268$$

$$x \approx 7.46$$ Rounded to two decimals.

Often, especially in application problems, you will not be told which ratio should be used to solve the problem. The following examples show how to decide whether to use $\sin \theta = \dfrac{\text{opp}}{\text{hyp}}$, $\cos \theta = \dfrac{\text{adj}}{\text{hyp}}$, or $\tan \theta = \dfrac{\text{opp}}{\text{adj}}$.

Example 4:

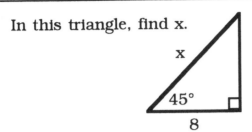

In this triangle, find x.

Solution: x = hyp and 8 = adj. In other words, the labeled sides in the above triangle are the **hypotenuse** and the **adjacent side**. The only ratio that involves **both** the hypotenuse and the adjacent side is the cosine ratio, namely $\cos = \dfrac{\text{adj}}{\text{hyp}}$. Therefore, we will use the cosine rather than the sine or the tangent.

$$\cos \theta = \frac{\text{adj}}{\text{hyp}}$$

$\cos 45° = \dfrac{8}{x}$ \qquad Since $\theta = 45°$, 8 = adj, x = hyp.

$0.707 = \dfrac{8}{x}$ \qquad From the table or a calculator.

$\dfrac{0.707}{1} = \dfrac{8}{x}$

$x = (1)(8) \div 0.707$ \quad Cross multiply and divide.

$x \approx 11.3$ \qquad Rounded to one decimal.

The next example is similar in that we must decide which ratio to use.

Example 5:

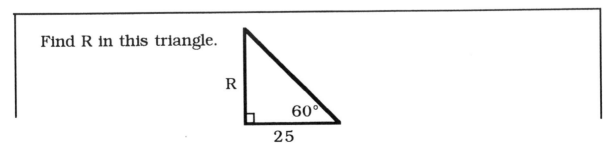

Find R in this triangle.

Solution: θ = 60°, 25 = adj, and R = opp.

The only ratio which involves both the **adjacent** and **opposite** sides is $\tan \theta = \frac{opp}{adj}$. Therefore, use the tangent rather than sine or cosine.

$$\tan \theta = \frac{opp}{adj}$$

$$\tan 60° = \frac{R}{25}$$

$$1.732 = \frac{R}{25} \qquad \text{By using table.}$$

$$\frac{1.732}{1} = \frac{R}{25}$$

$$R = (1.732)(25) + 1 = 43.3$$

Finding the Unknown Side. Exercise 2.

1. In each of the following use $\sin \theta = \frac{opp}{hyp}$ to solve for x (as in Example 1). Round answers to one decimal.

A.
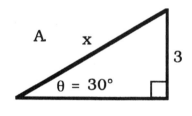

B.

C.
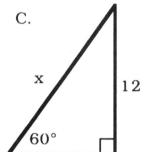

D.
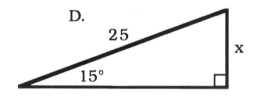

2. In each of the following use $\cos \theta = \frac{adj}{hyp}$ to find x (as in Example 2). Round to one decimal.

A.
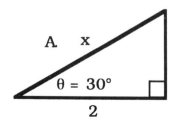

B.
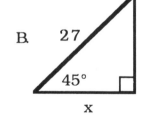

C.
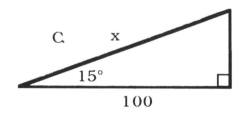

3. Use $\tan \theta = \dfrac{\text{opp}}{\text{adj}}$ to solve for x (as in Example 3). Round to one decimal.

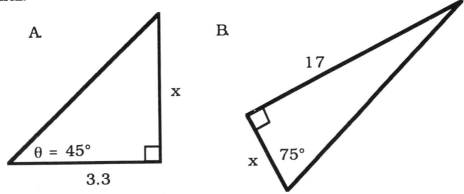

A.
$\theta = 45°$
3.3
x

B.
17
75°
x

4. Find x by first determining which ratio to use (as in Examples 4 and 5). Round to one decimal.

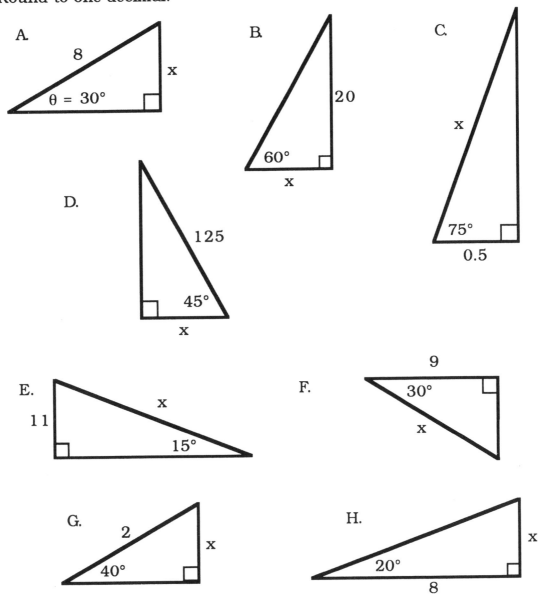

A.
8
x
$\theta = 30°$

B.
20
60°
x

C.
x
75°
0.5

D.
125
45°
x

E.
11
x
15°

F.
9
30°
x

G.
2
x
40°

H.
x
20°
8

Applications

The techniques demonstrated in the last section have widespread applications in science, engineering, surveying and navigation.

Example 1:

A surveyor is standing 100 yards from the base of a cliff. Using a machine that can measure angles, she has determined that the line of sight to the top of the cliff is 30° above the horizontal. How high is the cliff above eye level?

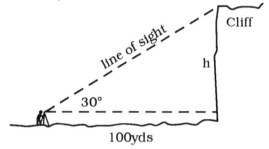

Solution: $\theta = 30°$, opp = h, adj = 100 yards.

$$\tan \theta = \frac{opp}{adj}$$

$$\tan 30° = \frac{h}{100}$$

$$0.577 = \frac{h}{100}$$

$$\frac{0.577}{1} = \frac{h}{100}$$

$$h = (0.577)(100) \div 1$$

$$h = 57.7 \text{ yards high}$$

The 30° angle in the above example is called an **angle of elevation**. This is because the surveyor's line of sight is <u>above</u> the horizontal. On the other hand, an angle is called an **angle of depression** if the surveyor's line of sight is <u>below</u> the horizontal. See Figure A and Figure B on the next page.

Figure A (looking upward)　　　Figure B (looking downward)

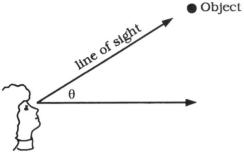

θ = angle of elevation

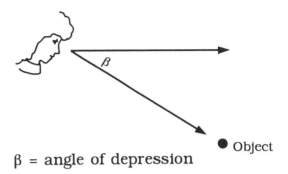

β = angle of depression

Example 2:

On a certain part of a roller coaster ride the track is straight and makes an angle of 45° with the horizontal. How far do the riders drop vertically while traveling 50 feet along this part of the track?

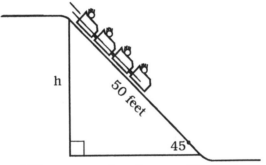

Solution: θ = 45°, opp = h, hyp = 50 feet.

$$\sin \theta = \frac{opp}{hyp}$$

$$\sin 45° = \frac{h}{50}$$

$$0.707 = \frac{h}{50}$$

$$\frac{0.707}{1} = \frac{h}{50}$$

$$h = (0.707)(50) \div 1 = 35.35 \text{ ft. drop}$$

Another way to interpret the previous example is to say that if you were riding this roller coaster and it was traveling along a track at the speed of 50 feet per second, then you would be dropping vertically at a speed of 35.35 feet per second.

Example 3:

An architect is designing a home in a town that gets a lot of rainfall. To avoid having too much standing water on it, the roof must have a 15° slope.

Assuming the distance from the center of the house to the outside wall is 40 feet, find the length of the roof part labeled x.

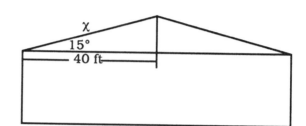

Solution: $\theta = 15°$,
adj = 40 ft.,
hyp = x .

$$\cos \theta = \frac{adj}{hyp}$$

$$\cos 15° = \frac{40}{x}$$

$$\frac{0.966}{1} = \frac{40}{x}$$

$$x = (40)(1) \div 0.966 = 41.4 \text{ ft. long}$$

Applications. Exercise 3. Round all answers to one decimal.

1. A surveyor standing 200 feet from the base of a tree has found that the angle of elevation to the top of the tree is 15°. Find the height of the tree.

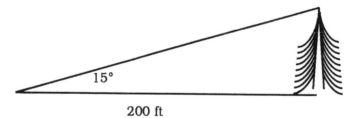

200 ft

2. Part of a roller coaster track is straight and makes an angle of 60° with the horizontal. How far does the roller coaster drop when it travels 74 feet along this track. (See Example 2 and draw a picture).

54

3. You are designing a house in a town that gets a lot of snow. You need the roof to have at least a 45° slope. How long must the roof be if it is 40 feet from the center of the house to the outside wall?

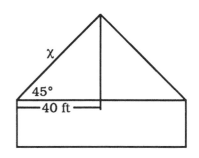

4. A certain mountain is known to be about 3 miles high. From your location, you notice that the angle of elevation to the top of the mountain is 15°. How far are you from the bottom of the mountain?

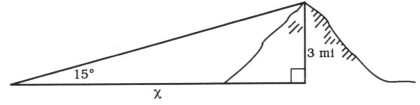

5. After hip surgery, a nurse elevated the patient's leg using a device that measures the degrees between the leg and the horizontal. If this device is set at 45° and if it is 12 inches from the patient's hip to knee, how high is the leg elevated?

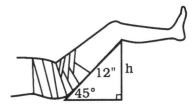

6. To find the width of a river, a surveyor has measured the angle between the bank that he is on and a tree on the other side. The angle is 75°. The surveyor also knows a 16 yard measure as shown below. Find the width of the river.

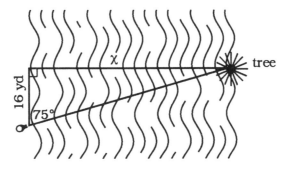

7. While riding in an airplane, you notice a city at an angle of depression of about 30°. If the airplane is 10,000 feet high, how far are you from the city?

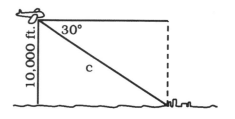

8. A photographer wishes to take a picture of a bird in a tree. She is 15 feet from the base of the tree and is shooting at a 50° angle of elevation. How far is the camera from the bird? (Hint: draw a picture)

9. A spy satellite 300 miles above earth spots a mobile missile launcher directly below. At an angle of 0.095° (θ), the satellite also sees a hospital. What is the distance between the missle launcher and the hospital? Hint: tan 0.095° ≈ 0.001658.

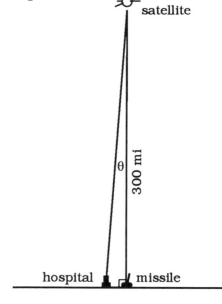

10. Consider location A and B on the surface of the earth, approximately 2085 miles apart. The angle of elevation to the moon from location A is θ= 89.5°.

Assuming that the moon is directly over location B, find the distance between the earth and the moon. Hint: Tan 89.5° ≈ 114.6.

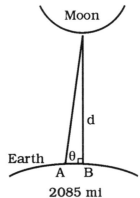

Finding an Unknown Angle

Whenever two sides of a right triangle are already known, then the angles can be found using the three trig ratios.

Example 1:

Find the measure of angles θ and β.

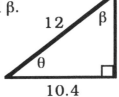

Solution: Let's choose to find θ first. The side labeled 10.4 is <u>adjacent</u> to θ. The <u>hypotenuse</u> is 12. Therefore, we will use the cosine ratio to find θ.

$$\cos \theta = \frac{adj}{hyp}$$
$$\cos \theta = \frac{10.4}{12}$$
$$\cos \theta \approx 0.867 \qquad \text{Since } 10.4 \div 12 \approx 0.867 \text{ (rounded)}.$$

Now use the table at the back of the book to find angle θ as in the previous chapter. Since the table is limited in scope, we must use the number in the cos θ column which comes closest to 0.867. In our table, that number is 0.866. To get a more precise answer, you must either use a calculator or a more comprehensive table.

Hence, θ ≈ 30°   Using our table.

Also, β ≈ 60°   Since all three angles must
                              add up to 180°. That is,
                              β + 30° + 90° = 180°.

Example 2:

A 5 foot tall woman casts a shadow 18.6 feet long.
What is the angle of elevation of the sun?

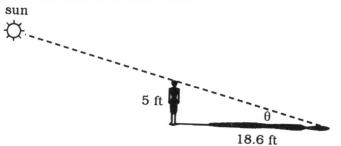

Solution: The labeled sides are opposite and adjacent to θ.
Therefore, we use the tangent ratio.

$$\tan \theta = \frac{opp}{adj}$$

$$\tan = \frac{5}{18.6}$$

$$\tan \theta \approx 0.269 \qquad \text{Divide 5 by 18.6, then rounding.}$$

The number that comes closest to 0.269 in the tan θ column
of our table is 0.268.

Hence, θ ≈ 15°

In other words, when the woman is casting her shadow, the
sun's elevation is approximately 15°.

In navigation (and surveying), the direction one is traveling is described
by the number of degrees away from north or south. For example, Figure A
below is labeled N 30° E, since that angle is 30° east of north.

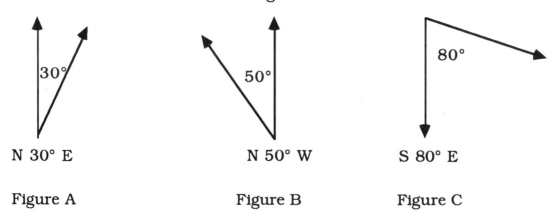

N 30° E	N 50° W	S 80° E
Figure A	Figure B	Figure C

Figure C is labeled S 80° E, since the angle is 80° east of south.

Example 3:

A navigator on a ship knows that he is 12 miles south of a lighthouse. He has a map which shows a port 5.6 miles east of the lighthouse. What direction should the ship travel in order to reach the port?

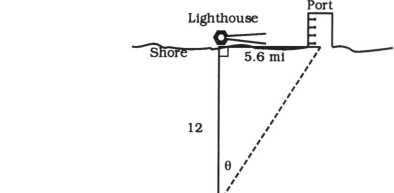

Solution: $\tan \theta = \dfrac{\text{opp}}{\text{adj}}$

$\tan \theta = \dfrac{5.6}{12}$

$\tan \theta \approx 0.467$ Since 5.6 ÷ 12 ≈ 0.467.

$\theta \approx 25°$ From a table or calculator.

Therefore, the ship should travel in the direction N 25° E.

Applications. Exercise 4.

1. In each of the following find θ and β as demonstrated in Example 1.

A.

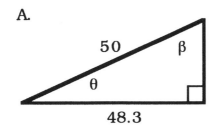

B.

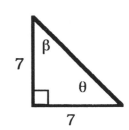

2. A 6 foot tall man casts a shadow 3.5 foot long. Find the angle of elevation of the sun. Hint: see Example 2. Also draw a picture.

3. While traveling 1000 feet along a straight declining road, a car experiences a vertical drop of 174 feet. Find angle θ .

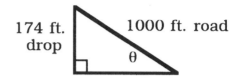

174 ft. drop   1000 ft. road   θ

4. A ship is 9 miles directly north of a lighthouse.. Which direction must the ship travel in order to reach a port that is 3.3 miles west of the lighthouse? Hint: Draw a picture.

5. A person in a wheelchair travels 30 feet along a ramp to reach an entrance that is 29 feet from the sidewalk. How steep is the ramp?

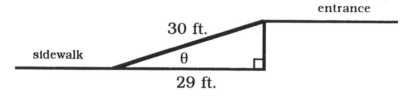

entrance

30 ft.

sidewalk   θ

29 ft.

6. While on a geology expedition, Greg and Kate have run out of water. The temperature is 101° Fahrenheit, and there are no trails. According to their map, the nearest water source could be reached by traveling 3 miles south, then 2.5 miles east. They have a compass. Which direction should they travel in order to reach the water source as quickly as possible?

7. Karen writes computer programs for a company that makes video games. In a particular game, she needs the triangle shown below to appear on the screen. In order to program the triangle into the software, it is necessary for her to know angle θ. Find θ.

10 cm.

θ

9.4 cm.

Review

Round all answers to one decimal.

1. Use $\sin \theta = \dfrac{\text{opp}}{\text{hyp}}$ to find x in this triangle.

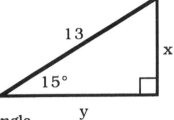

2. Use $\cos \theta = \dfrac{\text{adj}}{\text{hyp}}$ to find y in this same triangle.

3. Use sine, cosine, or tangent to find x in each triangle:

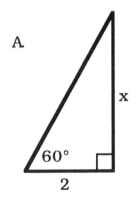

A.

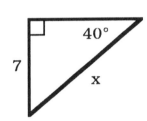

B.

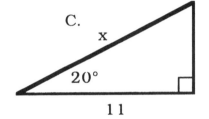

C.

4. At a place 50 feet away from the base of a tree, the angle of elevation is 40° to the top of the tree. How tall is the tree? (Hint: Draw a picture)

5. Find θ and β .

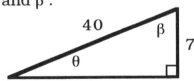

6. While traveling 120 feet along an off-ramp from the freeway, a car experiences a verticle drop of 41 feet. Find the angle of depression between the off-ramp and the freeway.

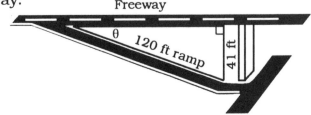

Chapter 1

1. Use this triangle to answer the following questions.

   A. Find the measure of θ.

   B. Which side is opposite θ?

   C. Which angle is opposite side R?

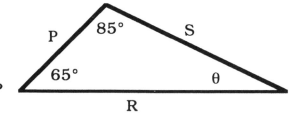

2. In each of the following, tell whether or not the triangle is a right triangle. If the triangle is right, then identify the hypotenuse and legs.

   A.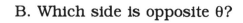

   B.

3. Find the length of the unknown side in each triangle.

   A.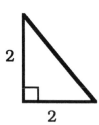

   B.

   C.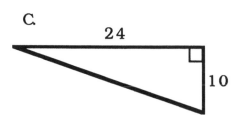

   D.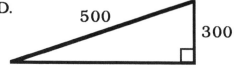

   E.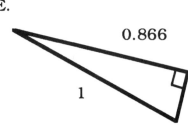

4. Write an appropriate formula for each triangle.

a.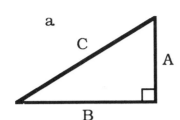

b.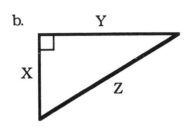

c.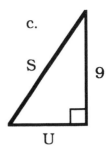

5. A surveyor has determined that a certain piece of property is in the shape of a right triangle. The legs measure 100 yards and 200 yards. Find the length of the third side.

Chapter 2

6. Use this triangle to find each of the following.

A. hyp =   D. sin θ=

B. opp =   E. cos θ=

C. adj =   F. tan θ=

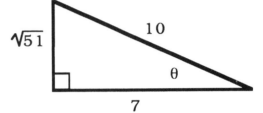

7. In each of the following find the sin α , cos α , and tan α .

A.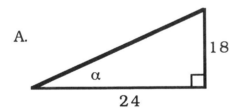

B.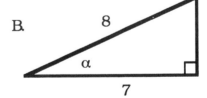

8. A small triangle inside a large triangle is shown below. Find the following:

A. sin θ using the small triangle.
B. sin θ using the large triangle.
C. tan θ using the small triangle.
D. tan θ using the large triangle.

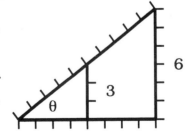

9. Use a table or calculator to find the following:

A. sin 20°   D. If tan α = 1, find α.

B. tan 80°   E. If cos β = 0.259, find β.

C. cos 45°   F. If sin θ = 0.707, find θ.

Chapter 3

10. Use the tangent ratio to find the
    length of side P in this triangle.

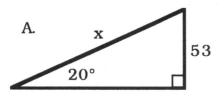

11. Use sine, cosine or tangent to find x in each triangle.

    A. 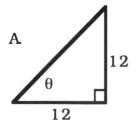   B.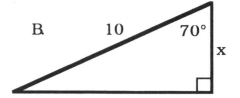

12. Find θ in each of the following.

    A.   B.

    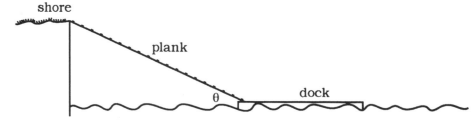

13. In a town in Alaska, a wooden plank is used to reach from the shore to a
    boat dock. At low tide the water level is 15 feet below the shore edge
    and the angle θ, between the plank and the water is, 40°. How long is
    the plank?

    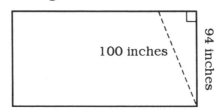

14. A saw in a mill can be set to cut plywood at specific angles. Assuming a
    sheet of plywood is 94 inches wide, at what angle should the saw be set
    in order for the cut edge (dotted line) to be 100 inches long?

Non-Right Triangles

This Appendix explains how to find unknown sides and unknown angles in non-right triangles. A non-right triangle is any triangle which does not contain a 90° angle.

The calculations of sine, cosine, and tangent for angles greater than 90° is beyond the scope of this book. Therefore, we will confine our discussion to triangles that contain only angles less than 90°. However, it should be noted that the following laws could be applied to triangles containing angles greater than 90°.

The Law of Sines

> In any triangle, if side A is opposite angle α and side B is opposite angle β ,
>
> then $\dfrac{\sin\alpha}{A} = \dfrac{\sin\beta}{B}$
>
>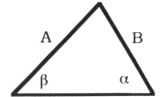

The following example shows how to use the formula $\dfrac{\sin\alpha}{A} = \dfrac{\sin\beta}{B}$ to find an unknown side.

Example 1:

> Use the formula $\dfrac{\sin\alpha}{A} = \dfrac{\sin\beta}{B}$ to calculate the length of side A.
>
>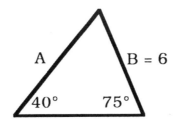

Answer: In the formula $\dfrac{\sin \alpha}{A} = \dfrac{\sin \beta}{B}$, α always represents the angle opposite side A. Therefore $\alpha = 75°$. Likewise, β always represents the angle opposite side B. Therefore, $\beta = 40°$. Moreover, side B is already known to be 6. Replacing α with 75°, β with 40°, and B with 6, we get:

$$\frac{\sin \alpha}{A} = \frac{\sin \beta}{B}$$

$$\frac{\sin 75°}{A} = \frac{\sin 40°}{B} \qquad \text{Since } \alpha = 75°, \ \beta = 40°, \ B = 6.$$

$$\frac{0.966}{A} = \frac{0.643}{6} \qquad \begin{array}{l}\text{Since } \sin 75° \approx 0.966 \text{ and} \\ \sin 40° = 0.643 \text{ by table or} \\ \text{calculator.}\end{array}$$

$$A = (6)(0.966) \div 0.643 \qquad \text{Cross multiply and divide.}$$
$$A \approx 9$$

When using the formula $\dfrac{\sin \alpha}{A} = \dfrac{\sin \beta}{B}$, it does not matter which two sides of the triangle are labeled as A or B. The main idea of the formula is that α is <u>opposite</u> Side A and β is <u>opposite</u> side B. Example 2 will emphasize this concept.

Example 2

Find the length of the side opposite the 70° angle.

Answer: Since the side opposite the 70° angle is not labeled, we can label it ourselves with "A" or "B" (It does not matter which letter we use). Let's choose to label it B.

The given side is 24, so A = 24.   70° is opposite B, so $\beta = 70°$. Also, 45° is opposite 24, so $\alpha = 45°$. Hence,

66

$$\frac{\sin \alpha}{A} = \frac{\sin \beta}{B}$$

$$\frac{\sin 45°}{24} = \frac{\sin 70°}{B}$$

Replacing A with 24, α with 45°, β with 70°

$$\frac{0.707}{24} = \frac{0.940}{B}$$

By using a table or calculator.

$$B = (24)(0.940) \div (0.707)$$

$$B \approx 31.9$$

The Law of Sines formula can also be used to find unknown angles.

Example 3

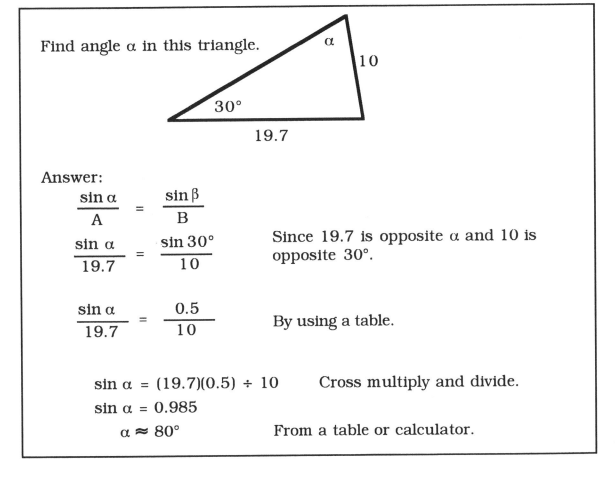

Find angle α in this triangle.

Answer:

$$\frac{\sin \alpha}{A} = \frac{\sin \beta}{B}$$

$$\frac{\sin \alpha}{19.7} = \frac{\sin 30°}{10}$$

Since 19.7 is opposite α and 10 is opposite 30°.

$$\frac{\sin \alpha}{19.7} = \frac{0.5}{10}$$

By using a table.

$$\sin \alpha = (19.7)(0.5) \div 10$$

Cross multiply and divide.

$$\sin \alpha = 0.985$$

$$\alpha \approx 80°$$

From a table or calculator.

In a more advanced course, it can be shown that the process in Example 3 sometimes leads to *ambiguous cases* , which are beyond the scope of this text.

Appendix. Exercise 1. Round all answers to one decimal.

1. For each triangle below, use $\dfrac{\sin \alpha}{A} = \dfrac{\sin \beta}{B}$ to find the unknown side labeled A or B (as Example 1).

a.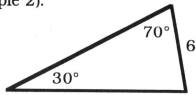

b.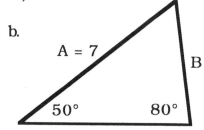

c.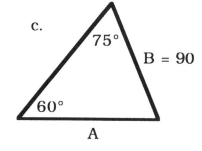

2. In the triangle below, find the side opposite the 70° angle (as in Example 2).

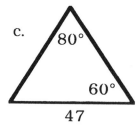

3. In each triangle, find the side opposite the 60° angle. (Hint: Example 2)

a.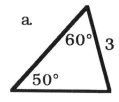

b.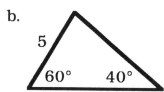

c.

4. In each triangle below, use $\dfrac{\sin \alpha}{A} = \dfrac{\sin \beta}{B}$ to find the unknown angles.
(Hint: Example 3)

a.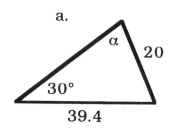

b.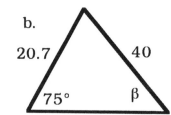

c.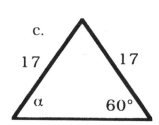

Law of Sines and Applications

You are already familiar with the formula $\dfrac{\sin \alpha}{A} = \dfrac{\sin \beta}{B}$. This section shows how to write similar formulas when the sides are labeled with letters other than A or B and the angles are labeled with letters other than α or β .

Example 1:

Write an appropriate Law of Sines formula for this triangle.

Solution: Angle γ is opposite side Y. Also, angle θ is opposite side X. Therefore,

$$\frac{\sin \gamma}{Y} = \frac{\sin \theta}{X}$$

Next we give an example of an application of the Law of Sines.

Example 2:

A surveyor is measuring a triangular shaped piece of property. He has already determined the length of one side and two angles as shown. What is the length of side P?

Solution: P is opposite 60°. Also 200 yards is opposite 40°. Therefore,

$$\frac{\sin 60°}{P} = \frac{\sin 40°}{200} \qquad \text{By the Law of Sines.}$$

$$\frac{0.866}{P} = \frac{0.643}{200}$$

From a table.

$$P = (0.866)(200) + 0.643$$

Cross multiply and divide.

$$P \approx 269 \text{ yards}$$

Appendix. Exercise 2.

1. Write appropriate Laws of Sines formulas for each.

a. 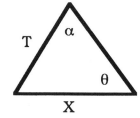 b. 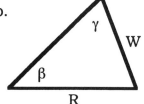 c.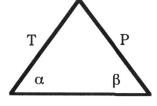

2. A surveyor wants to know the length of a swamp. She has already determined the angles and side shown below. How long is the swamp?

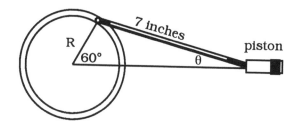

3. A 7 inch shaft connects a piston to a wheel as shown. The wheel radius, R, equals 2.09 inches. Find θ when the wheel is turned 60° (as shown).

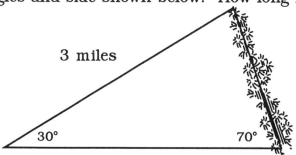

Law of Cosines

The unknown sides and angles in the figures below can not be found using the Law of Sines. This is because the Law of Sines only works when one angle **and** the side opposite that angle are both given.

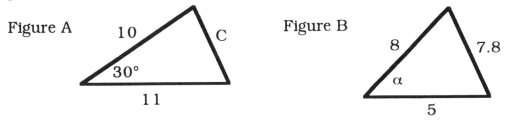

Figure A   Figure B

In such cases we must use the Law of Cosines.

Law of Cosines

In <u>any</u> triangle, if the sides are A, B, and C, and if C is <u>opposite</u> angle θ then, $C^2 = A^2 + B^2 - 2AB \cos \theta$.

Example 1 below shows how to use the Law of Cosines formula to find side C in Figure A above.

Example 1

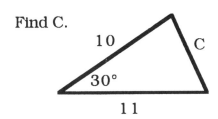

Find C.

Answer: 30° is opposite side C, therefore θ = 30°. The known sides are 10 and 11. We can replace A and B with 10 and 11 (in any order) and θ with 30° to get:

$$C^2 = A^2 + B^2 - 2 \; A \; B \; \cos \theta$$
$$C^2 = 10^2 + 11^2 - 2(10)(11) \cos 30°$$
$$C^2 = 100 + 121 - 220 \cos 30°$$
$$C^2 = 221 - 220 \; (0.866) \qquad \text{From table.}$$
$$C^2 = 221 - 190.52$$
$$C^2 = 30.48$$
$$C = \sqrt{30.48} \approx 5.5 \qquad \text{From a calculator.}$$

The next example shows how to find α in Figure B.

Example 2:

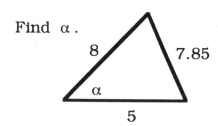

Find α.

8   7.85

α

5

Answer: 7.85 is opposite α , therefore C = 7.85.

$$C^2 = A^2 + B^2 - 2 \; A \; B \; \cos \alpha$$
$$(7.85)^2 = 8^2 + 5^2 - 2(8)(5) \cos \alpha$$
$$61.6225 = 64 + 25 - 80 \cos \alpha$$
$$61.6225 = 89 - 80 \cos \alpha$$
$$61.6225 - 89 = -80 \cos \alpha \qquad \text{Subtraction Principle.}$$
$$-27.3775 = -80 \cos \alpha$$
$$0.342 = \cos \alpha \qquad \text{By dividing -27.3775 by -80}$$
and rounding to three decimals.

Therefore α ≈ 70°   From table.

Appendix. Exercise 3.

1. Use the Law of Cosines to find C in each (Hint: Example 1):

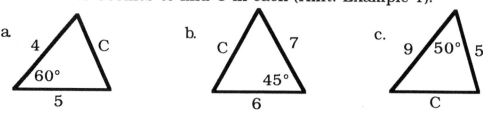

a.
4   C
60°
5

b.
C   7
45°
6

c.
9 50° 5
C

2. In each figure find α as show in Example 2:

a.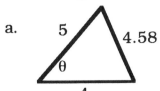

b.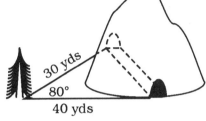

c.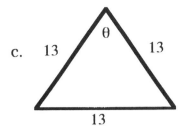

3. Engineers are planning to build a tunnel through a hill. They already know that it is 30 yards from one side of the hill to a nearby tree. Also, the distance from the tree to the other side of the hill is 40 yards and the angle between these distance is 80°. Find the length of the tunnel when it is completed.

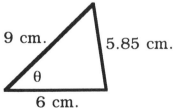

4. A triangular piece of land has sides measuring 700 feet, 500 feet, and 747.5 feet. Find angle θ .

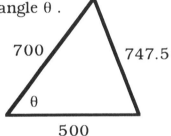

5. Brandon is writing a computer program that displays geometric shapes for architectural drawings. His program needs to include a triangle with sides measuring 6 cm., 9 cm. and 5.85 cm. In order to incorporate this triangle into the software, he needs to know the angles in the triangle. Find θ .

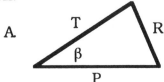

6. We have used $C^2 = A^2 + B^2 - 2AB \cos \theta$ where C is opposite angle θ, and A and B are adjacent to θ . Write an appropriate Law of Cosines formula for each.

A.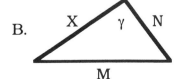

B.

73

ANSWERS

Skills Review. Page 1. Exercise 1.
1. 0.75
2. 0.3125
3. 0.625
4. 0.48
5. 22.98 (rounded to two decimals)

Skills Review. Page 2. Exercise 2.
1. right
2. acute
3. obtuse
4. acute
5. acute
6. right

Skills Review. Page 2. Exercise 3.
1. $x = 3$
2. $Y = 8$
3. $x = 5$
4. $A = 11$
5. $B = 51$
6. $B = 46$

Skills Review. Page 3. Exercise 4.
1. A. $0.237 \approx 0.24$
   B. 15.31
   C. 180.02
2. A. 4.2
   B. 79.6
   C. 8.6

Skills Review. Page 4. Exercise 5.
A. 2
B. 5
C. 10
D. 1
E. $\sqrt{3} \approx 1.73$
F. $\sqrt{5} \approx 2.24$
G. $\sqrt{11} \approx 3.32$
H. 9

Skills Review. Page 5. Exercise 6.
1. $x = 3$
2. $x = 5$
3. $4 = x$ or $x = 4$
4. $x = \sqrt{7}$ or $x \approx 2.65$
5. $c = 2$
6. $6 = c$
7. $c = \sqrt{15} \approx 3.87$
8. $A = 8$
9. $B = \sqrt{10} \approx 3.16$

Chapter 1. Page 8. Exercise 1.
1. 180°
2. A. 60°
   B. 50°
   C. 40°
   D. 30°
3. A. α
   B. C
   C. β
   D. θ
   E. Z
   F. γ
4. A. angles
   B. sides
5. A. θ
   B. The 90° angle.
   C. 60°
   D. 30°

Chapter 1. Page 11. Exercise 2.
1. Triangles B, D, and E.
2.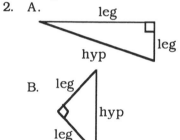
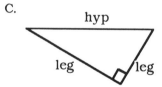
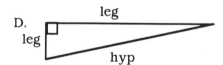
3. A. leg
   B. leg
   C. hypotenuse
   D. Y
4. A. $\sqrt{10}$
   B. 3 and 1
5. A. opposite
   B. hypotenuse
   C. 1. 10
      2. 6 and 8
      3. $10^2 = \mathbf{100}$
      4. $6^2 = \mathbf{36}$, $8^2 = \mathbf{64}$
      5. $36 + 64 = \mathbf{100}$
      6. yes.

74

ANSWERS

Chapter 1. Page 15. Exercise 3.
1. A. C = 5
   Hint: $C^2 = A^2 + B^2$
   $C^2 = 3^2 + 4^2$
   $C^2 = 9 + 16$
   $C^2 = 25$
   $C = \sqrt{25} = 5$
   B. $C = \sqrt{29} \approx 5.39$
   C. $C = \sqrt{5} \approx 2.24$
   D. C = 25
   E. $C = \sqrt{2} \approx 1.41$
   F. C = 15
2. yes

Chapter 1. Page 17. Exercise 4.
1. A. B = 4
   Hint: $C^2 = A^2 + B^2$
   $5^2 = 3^2 + B^2$
   $25 = 9 + B^2$
   $25 - 9 = B^2$
   $16 = B^2$
   $\sqrt{16} = B$
   $4 = B$
   B. $A = \sqrt{13}$ or 3.61
   C. $A = \sqrt{15}$
   D. 12
   E. $\sqrt{3}$
   F. $A = \sqrt{12.48} \approx 3.53$

Chapter 1. Page 19. Exercise 5.
1. A. $T^2 = U^2 + V^2$ or $T^2 = V^2 + U^2$
   B. $A^2 = E^2 + I^2$
   C. $5^2 = H^2 + W^2$
   D. $C^2 = A^2 + B^2$
   E. $A^2 = C^2 + B^2$, Hint: A = hyp
2. A. $K^2 = 8^2 + 6^2$; K = 10
   B. $6^2 = X^2 + 4^2$; $X = \sqrt{20}$
   C. $Y^2 = 3^2 + 3^2$; $Y = \sqrt{18}$
   D. $5^2 = 1^2 + P^2$; $P = \sqrt{24}$
   E. $W^2 = 20^2 + 10^2$; $W = \sqrt{500}$
   F. $41^2 = C^2 + 9^2$; C = 40

Chapter 1. Page 22. Exercise 6.
1. C = 13 yd
2. $\sqrt{96} \approx 9.80$ miles
3. $\sqrt{257} \approx 16.03$ ft.
4. $\sqrt{75} \approx 8.66$ min.
5. Yes, since only about 39 ft. is needed.

Chapter 1. Review. Page 24.
1. A. 50°
   B. 35°
2. A. α
   B. 10 cm.
   C. 45°
3. Triangle B only.
4. A. E
   B. F and D
5. A. C = 5
   B. $\sqrt{53}$
   C. A = 6
   D. $\sqrt{56}$
   E. X = 13
   F. $Y = \sqrt{40}$
6. $G^2 = H^2 + V^2$
7. $\sqrt{221} \approx 14.87$ ft.
   Hint: Draw a picture.

Chapter 2. Page 26. Exercise 1.
1. $\frac{4}{9}$
2. $\frac{P}{T}$
3. A. $\frac{8}{2} = 4$
   B. $\frac{1}{4}$
   C. $\frac{2}{5}$

Hint: perimeter = 8 + 2 + 8 + 2 = 20

Chapter 2. Page 29. Exercise 2.
1. A. opp = 3, adj = 4, hyp = 5
   B. opp = $\sqrt{5}$, adj = 2, hyp = 3
   C. opp = Y, adj = X, hyp = Z
   D. opp = L, adj = K, hyp = M
2. A. 10 miles
   B. P
   C. 7 miles
   D. adjacent, opposite
   E. $\sqrt{51}$

Chapter 2. Page 33. Exercise 3.
1. A. $\sin \theta = \frac{5}{13}$, $\cos \theta = \frac{12}{13}$, $\tan \theta = \frac{5}{12}$
   B. $\sin \theta = \frac{6}{10} = \frac{3}{5}$, $\cos \theta = \frac{4}{5}$, $\tan \theta = \frac{3}{4}$
   C. $\sin \theta = \frac{\sqrt{13}}{7}$, $\cos \theta = \frac{2}{7}$, $\tan \theta = \frac{\sqrt{13}}{2}$
   D. $\sin \theta = \frac{40}{41}$, $\cos \theta = \frac{9}{41}$, $\tan \theta = \frac{40}{9}$

Hint: θ is in the upper left corner.

ANSWERS

E. $\sin \theta = \dfrac{1}{\sqrt{5}}$, $\cos \theta = \dfrac{2}{\sqrt{5}}$, $\tan \theta = \dfrac{1}{2}$

F. $\sin \theta = \dfrac{3}{\sqrt{18}}$, $\cos \theta = \dfrac{3}{\sqrt{18}}$, $\tan \theta = \dfrac{3}{3} = 1$

2. A. $\sin \alpha = \dfrac{\sqrt{3}}{2}$, $\cos \alpha = \dfrac{1}{2}$, $\tan \alpha = \dfrac{\sqrt{3}}{1} = \sqrt{3}$

B. $\sin \alpha = \dfrac{\sqrt{15}}{4}$, $\cos \alpha = \dfrac{1}{4}$, $\tan \alpha = \sqrt{15}$

C. $\sin \alpha = \dfrac{2}{\sqrt{13}}$, $\cos \alpha = \dfrac{3}{\sqrt{13}}$, $\tan \alpha = \dfrac{2}{3}$

3. $\sin \alpha = \dfrac{\sqrt{3}}{2} \approx 0.866$, $\cos \alpha = 0.5$,

$\tan \alpha \approx 1.732$

4. A. $\sin 50° = \dfrac{1.532}{2} = 0.766$

B. $\cos 50° = 0.643$

C. $\tan 50° = \dfrac{1.532}{1.286} \approx 1.191$

D. 0.643

E. 0.766

F. 40°

5. Trigonometric ratios.

Chapter 2. Page 37. Exercise 4.

1. A. $\cos = \dfrac{4}{5}$

B. $\cos = \dfrac{9}{15} = \dfrac{4}{5}$

C. Fact 2: The triangle size does not affect the cosine ratio.

2. A. $\dfrac{3}{4}$

B. $\dfrac{9}{12} = \dfrac{3}{4}$

C. Fact 3 on page 36.

3. A. $\dfrac{5}{13}$

B. $\dfrac{10}{26} = \dfrac{5}{13}$

C. $\dfrac{12}{13}$

D. $\dfrac{24}{26} = \dfrac{12}{13}$

E. Small triangle $\tan \theta = \dfrac{5}{12}$

Large triangle $\tan \theta = \dfrac{10}{24} = \dfrac{5}{12}$

F. The size of the triangle has no affect on the sine, cosine, or tangent ratios.

4. A. $\tan = \dfrac{1}{1} = 1$

B. $\tan = \dfrac{1.25}{1.25} = 1$

C. $\dfrac{2}{2} = 1$

D. Fact 3

5. A. hyp = $2 \frac{1}{2}$ in, opp = $1 \frac{1}{4}$ in

B. hyp = 2.5 in, opp = 1.25 in

C. Yes, $\sin 30° = \dfrac{1.25}{2.5} = 0.5$

6. A. Triangle A hyp $\approx$ 1.414

Triangle B hyp $\approx$ 1.768

Triangle C hyp $\approx$ 2.828

B. Triangle A $\cos 45° = \dfrac{1}{1.414} \approx 0.707$

Triangle B $\cos 45° \approx 0.707$

Triangle C $\cos 45° \approx 0.707$

C. Fact 2

Chapter 2. Page 40. Exercise 5.

1. A. 0.174   G. 0.966

B. 0.176   H. 1.192

C. 0.707   I. 0.5

D. 5.671   J. 0.5

E. 0.259   K. 0.866

F. 0.966   L. 3.732

2. A. 15°   E. 80°

B. 30°   F. 20°

C. 45°   G. 70°

D. 45°   H. 20°

3. The entries in the $\cos \theta$ column are the same as in the $\sin \theta$ column except that they are in reverse order.

Chapter 2. Page 42. Exercise 6.

1. A. 0.707   2. A. 75.0°

B. 1.192   B. 84.0°

C. 0.999   C. 89.5°

D. 0.017

E. 0.222

F. 0.002

ANSWERS

Chapter 2. Review. Page 43.

1. A. opp = 8, adj = 6, hyp = 10

    B. opp = $\sqrt{11}$, adj = 5, hyp = 6

2. A. $\sin\theta = \dfrac{4}{5}$, $\cos\theta = \dfrac{3}{5}$, $\tan\theta = \dfrac{4}{3}$

    B. $\sin\theta = \dfrac{\sqrt{11}}{6}$, $\cos\theta = \dfrac{5}{6}$, $\tan\theta = \dfrac{\sqrt{11}}{5}$

3. A. $\dfrac{3}{5}$

    B. $\dfrac{4}{5}$

    C. $\dfrac{3}{4}$

    D. $\dfrac{4}{5}$

4. 0.5

5. A. size

    B. triangle

6. A. 0.174   D. 0.707

    B. 0.174   E. 0.707

    C. 1   F. 2.747

7. A. $\theta \approx 80°$

    B. $\theta \approx 45°$

    C. $\alpha \approx 20°$

8. A. $\dfrac{3}{5}$

    B. $\dfrac{3}{5}$

    C. $\dfrac{4}{5}$ each

    D. $\dfrac{3}{4}$ each

9. A. $\dfrac{x}{z}$ D. $\dfrac{y}{z}$

    B. $\dfrac{x}{z}$ E. $\dfrac{x}{y}$

    C. $\dfrac{y}{z}$ F. $\dfrac{y}{x}$

Chapter 3. Page 46. Exercise 1.

1. A. x = 3   E. x = 0.2

    B. y = 2.8   F. x = 3.5

    C. x = 4   G. P ≈ 5.66

    D. c = 2   H. y ≈ 2.75

                 I. x = 25

Chapter 3. Page 50. Exercise 2.

1. A. x = 6

    B. x ≈ 2.8

    Hint: $\sin 45° = \dfrac{x}{4}$

    $0.707 = \dfrac{x}{4}$

    $\dfrac{0.707}{1} = \dfrac{x}{4}$

    $x = (0.707)(4) \div 1 \approx 2.8$

    C. 13.9

    D. 6.5

2. A. x ≈ 2.3

    Hint : $\cos 30° = \dfrac{2}{x}$

    B. 19.1

    C. 103.5

3. A. 3.3

    Hint: $\tan 45° = \dfrac{x}{3.3}$

    $1 = \dfrac{x}{3.3}$

    $\dfrac{1}{1} = \dfrac{x}{3.3}$

    $x = (1)(3.3) \div 1$

    B. 4.6

4. A. 4 (use sine)

    B. 11.5 ($\tan 60° = \dfrac{20}{x}$)

    C. 1.9 (use cosine)

    D. 88.4 (use cosine)

    E. 42.5

    F. 10.4

    G. 1.3

    H. 2.9

Chapter 3. Page 54. Exercise 3.

1. 53.6 ft. (see Example 1)

2. 64.1 ft. drop

   Hint:

   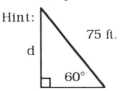

ANSWERS

3. 56.6 ft. (see Example 3)

4. 11.2 miles

5. 8.5 in.

6. 59.7 yd. (use tangent)

7. 20,000 ft. $\left(\sin 30° = \dfrac{10,000}{x}\right)$

8. 23.3 ft.

Hint: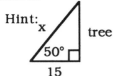

9. 0.5 miles $\left(\tan 0.095° = \dfrac{x}{300}\right)$

10. 239,000 miles (rounded to the nearest thousandth).

Chapter 3. Page 59. Exercise 4.

1. A. $\theta = 15°$ $\beta = 75°$

    B. $\theta = 45°$ $\beta = 45°$

    Hint: $\tan \theta = \dfrac{7}{7}$

    $\tan \theta = 1$

2. About 60° since $\dfrac{6}{3.5} \approx 1.71$ comes closest to 1.732 in the tan θ column (or by calculator).

3. $\theta \approx 10°$

4. About S 20° W

    Hint: See Example 3.

5. $\theta \approx 15°$

6. About S 40° E

    Hint: Draw a picture.

7. $\theta = 20°$

Chapter 3. Review. Page 61.

1. 3.4 rounded

2. 12.6

3. A. 3.5

    B. 10.9

    C. 11.7

4. 42.0 ft.

5. $\theta \approx 10°$, $\beta \approx 80°$ (use sine)

6. $\theta \approx 20°$

Cumulative Review Chapter 1- 3. Page 62.

1. A. 30°

    B. P

    C. 85°

2. A. Not a right triangle.

    B. Right; hyp = G, legs are A and F.

3. A. $\sqrt{8}$

    B. $\sqrt{5}$

    C. 26

    D. 400

    E. 0.5

4. A. $C^2 = A^2 + B^2$

    B. $Z^2 = X^2 + Y^2$

    C. $S^2 = U^2 + 9^2$

5. $\sqrt{50,000} \approx 223.6$ yd.

6. A. 10   D. $\dfrac{\sqrt{51}}{10}$

    B. $\sqrt{51}$ E. $\dfrac{7}{10}$

    C. 7   F. $\dfrac{\sqrt{51}}{7}$

7. A. $\sin \alpha = \dfrac{18}{30} = \dfrac{3}{5}$

    $\cos \alpha = \dfrac{4}{5}$

    $\tan \alpha = \dfrac{3}{4}$

    B. $\sin \alpha = \dfrac{\sqrt{15}}{8}$

    $\cos \alpha = \dfrac{7}{8}$

    $\tan \alpha = \dfrac{\sqrt{15}}{7}$

8. A. $\dfrac{3}{5}$ C. $\dfrac{3}{4}$

    B. $\dfrac{3}{5}$ D. $\dfrac{3}{4}$

9. A. 0.342   D. 45°

    B. 5.671   E. 75°

    C. 0.707   F. 45°

10. 14.4 (rounded)

11. A. 155.0

    B. 3.4

ANSWERS

12. A. 45°
    B. 80°
13. 23.3 ft.
14. 20°

6. A. $R^2 = T^2 + P^2 - 2TP \cos \beta$
   B. $M^2 = X^2 + N^2 - 2XN \cos \gamma$

Appendix. Page 68. Exercise 1.

1. A. 7.3
   B. 5.4
   Hint: $\alpha = 80°$
   C. 100.4
2. 11.3
3. A. 3.4
   B. 6.7
   C. 41.3
4. A. 80°
   B. $\beta \approx 30°$
   C. 60°

Appendix. Page 70. Exercise 2.

1. A. $\dfrac{\sin \alpha}{X} = \dfrac{\sin \theta}{T}$
   B. $\dfrac{\sin \beta}{W} = \dfrac{\sin \gamma}{R}$
   C. $\dfrac{\sin \alpha}{P} = \dfrac{\sin \beta}{T}$
2. 1.6 miles
3. $\theta \approx 15°$

Appendix. Page 72. Exercise 3.

1. A. $\sqrt{21} \approx 4.6$
   B. 5.1 rounded
   C. 6.9
2. A. $\theta \approx 60°$
   B. 45°
   Hint: C = 7.33
   C. 60°
3. 45.6 yd.
4. 75°
5. 40°

79

Math Series

GarlicPress
Tools for Learning and Growing

The Straight Forward Math Series

is systematic, first diagnosing skill levels, then *practice*, periodic *review*, and *testing*.

Blackline

GP-006 Addition
GP-012 Subtraction
GP-007 Multiplication
GP-013 Division
GP-039 Fractions
GP-083 Word Problems, Book 1
GP-042 Word Problems, Book 2

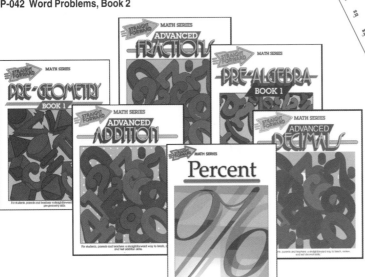

The Advanced Straight Forward Math Series

is a higher level system to diagnose, practice, review, and test skills.

Blackline

GP-015 Advanced Addition
GP-016 Advanced Subtraction
GP-017 Advanced Multiplication
GP-018 Advanced Division
GP-020 Advanced Decimals
GP-021 Advanced Fractions
GP-044 Mastery Tests
GP-025 Percent
GP-028 Pre-Algebra, Book 1
GP-029 Pre-Algebra, Book 2
GP-030 Pre-Geometry, Book 1
GP-031 Pre-Geometry, Book 2

Upper Level Math Series

GP-104 Algebra, Book 1
GP-105 Algebra, Book 2
GP-045 Trigonometry
GP-054 Geometry
GP-053 Pre-Calculus
GP-064 Calculus AB, Vol. 1
GP-067 Calculus AB, Vol. 2

2 SIDED Self-Checking Math Puzzles

Each puzzle set contains 10 individual puzzles. Each six-inch puzzle is two-sided. One side contains basic math facts, the other side has a photograph. Each puzzle has its own clear plastic tray and lid.

Math problems are solved in the bottom tray (answer pieces are all the same shape). The lid is closed and the puzzle is turned over. If the photo is jumbled, the math facts have not been completed correctly.

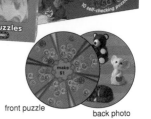

GP-113 Addition Puzzles
GP-114 Subtraction Puzzles
GP-115 Multiplication Puzzles
GP-116 Division Puzzles
GP-122 Multiplication & Division Puzzles
GP-123 Money Puzzles

front puzzle   back photo

ENGLISH SERIES

The **Straight Forward English** series is designed to measure, teach, review, and master specific English skills. All pages are reproducible and include answers to exercises and tests.

Capitalization & Punctuation
GP-032 • 40 pages
I and First Words; Proper Nouns; Ending Marks and Sentences; Commas; Apostrophes; Quotation Marks.

Nouns & Pronouns
GP-033 • 40 pages
Singular and Plural Nouns; Common and Proper Nouns; Concrete and Abstract Nouns; Collective Nouns; Possessive Pronouns; Pronouns and Contractions; Subject and Object Pronouns.

Verbs
GP-034 • 40 pages
Action Verbs; Linking Verbs; Verb Tense; Subject-Verb Agreement; Spelling Rules for Tense; Helping Verbs; Irregular Verbs; Past Participles.

Sentences
GP-041 • 40 pages
Sentences; Subject and Predicate; Sentence Structures.

Adjectives & Adverbs
GP-035 • 40 pages
Proper Adjectives; Articles; Demonstrative Adjectives; Comparative Adjectives; Special Adjectives: Good and Bad; -ly Adverbs; Comparative Adverbs; Good-Well and Bad-Badly.

Prepositions, Conjunctions and Interjections
GP-043 • 40 pages
Recognizing Prepositions; Object of the Preposition; Prepositional Phrases; Prepositional Phrases as Adjectives and Adverbs; Faulty Reference; Coordinating, Correlative and Subordinate Conjunctions.

ADVANCED ENGLISH SERIES

Get It Right!
GP-148 • 144 pages
Organized into four sections, **Get It Right!** is designed to teach writing skills commonly addressed in the standardized testing in the early grades: Spelling, Mechanics, Usage, and Proofreading. Overall the book includes 100 lessons, plus reviews and skill checks.

All-In-One English
GP-107 • 112 pages
The **All-In-One** is a master book to the Straight Forward English Series.
Under one cover it has included the important English skills of capitalization, punctuation, and all eight parts of speech. Each selection of the All-In-One explains and models a skill and then provides focused practice, periodic review, and testing to help measure acquired skills. Progress through all skills is thorough and complete.

Grammar Rules!
GP-102 • 250 pages
Grammar Rules! is a straightforward approach to basic English grammar and English writing skills. Forty units each composed of four lessons for a total of 160 lessons, plus review, skill checks, and answers. Units build skills with Parts of Speech, Mechanics, Diagramming, and Proofreading. Solid grammar and writing skills are explained, modeled, practiced, reviewed, and tested.

Clauses & Phrases
GP-055 • 80 pages
Adverb, Adjective and Noun Clauses; Gerund, Participial and Infinitive Verbals; Gerund, Participial, Infinitive, Prepositional and Appositive Phrases.

Mechanics
GP-056 • 80 pages
Abbreviations; Apostrophes; Capitalization; Italics; Quotation Marks; Numbers; Commas; Semicolons; Colons; Hyphens; Parentheses; Dashes; Brackets; Ellipses; Slashes.

Grammar & Diagramming Sentences
GP-075 • 110 pages
The Basics; Diagramming Rules and Patterns; Pronouns; Verbs; Modifiers; Prepositions, Conjunctions, and Special Items; Clauses and Compound-Complex Sentences.

Troublesome Grammar
GP-019 • 120 pages •
Agreement; Regular and Irregular Verbs; Modifiers; Prepositions and Case, Possessives and Contractions; Plurals; Active and Passive Voice;